# West Coast Wrecks

# &

# Other Maritime Tales

*Rick James*

HARBOUR PUBLISHING

**Harbour Publishing Co. Ltd.**
P.O. Box 219, Madeira Park, BC, V0N 2H0
www.harbourpublishing.com

Cover painting by Peter Rindlisbacher
Edited by Ian Whitelaw
Cover design by Teresa Karbashewski
Text design by Mary White
Index by Natalia Cornwall
Printed and bound in Canada

Harbour Publishing acknowledges financial support from the Government of Canada through the Canada Book Fund and the Canada Council for the Arts, and from the Province of British Columbia through the BC Arts Council and the Book Publishing Tax Credit.

**Library and Archives Canada Cataloguing in Publication**

James, Rick, 1947–
      Raincoast chronicles 21 : west coast wrecks and other maritime tales / Rick James.

Includes index.
ISBN 978-1-55017-545-5

      1. Shipwrecks—British Columbia—History. 2. Ships—British Columbia—History. 3. Seafaring life—British Columbia—History. 4. British Columbia—History. I. Title. II. Title: Raincoast chronicles twenty-one. III. Title: West coast wrecks and other maritime tales.

FC3820.S5J36 2011                 971.1                 C2011-904505-2

*To my mentor and in-house editor, Paula Wild,*
*who remained always patient and understanding*
*while going over innumerable drafts with a critical eye*
*over the past twenty years.*

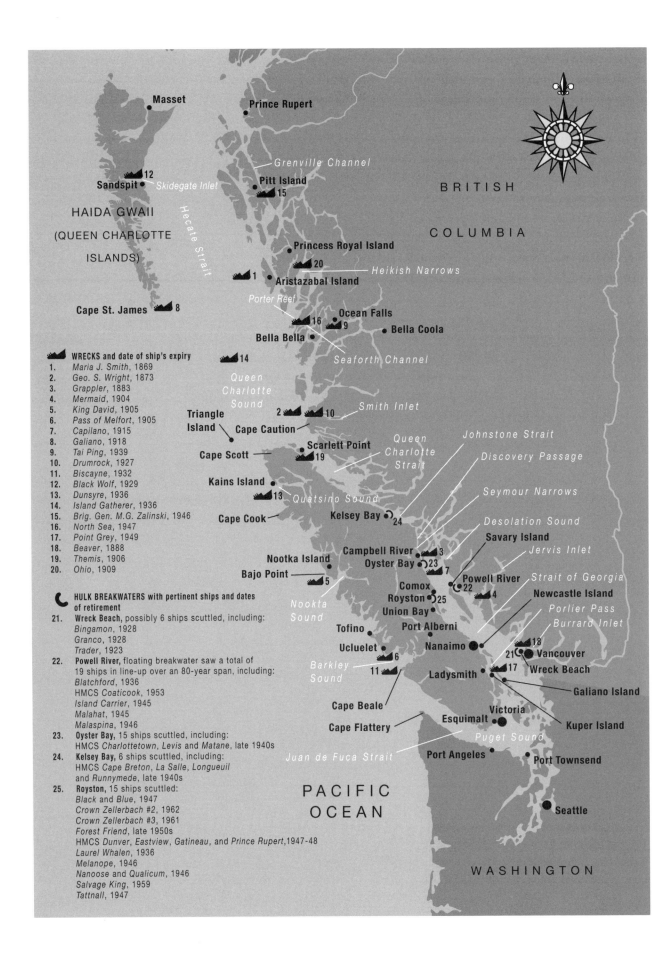

Masset

Prince Rupert

*Grenville Channel*

Sandspit ◄12 *Skidegate Inlet*

Pitt Island
◄15

*Hecate Strait*

HAIDA GWAII
(QUEEN CHARLOTTE
ISLANDS)

BRITISH

COLUMBIA

Princess Royal Island

◄20

*Heikish Narrows*

◄1
Aristazabal Island

Cape St. James ◄8

*Porter Reef*

◄16    Ocean Falls
          9

Bella Bella

*Seaforth Channel*

Bella Coola

◄14

*Queen
Charlotte
Sound*

WRECKS and date of ship's expiry
1.    *Maria J. Smith*, 1869
2.    *Geo. S. Wright*, 1873
3.    *Grappler*, 1883
4.    *Mermaid*, 1904
5.    *King David*, 1905
6.    *Pass of Melfort*, 1905
7.    *Capilano*, 1915
8.    *Galiano*, 1918
9.    *Tai Ping*, 1939
10.  *Drumrock*, 1927
11.  *Biscayne*, 1932
12.  *Black Wolf*, 1929
13.  *Dunsyre*, 1936
14.  *Island Gatherer*, 1936
15.  *Brig. Gen. M.G. Zalinski*, 1946
16.  *North Sea*, 1947
17.  *Point Grey*, 1949
18.  *Beaver*, 1888
19.  *Themis*, 1906
20.  *Ohio*, 1909

2 ◄ ◄10    *Smith Inlet*

Triangle
Island
Cape Caution

*Johnstone Strait*

Scarlett Point

*Discovery Passage*

Cape Scott    19

*Queen
Charlotte
Strait*

*Seymour Narrows*

Kains Island

13

*Quatsino Sound*

*Desolation Sound*

Kelsey Bay ◐24

Savary Island

Cape Cook

Campbell River    3
Oyster Bay    ◐23    7

*Jervis Inlet*

HULK BREAKWATERS with pertinent ships and dates
of retirement
21.    **Wreck Beach**, possibly 6 ships scuttled, including:
         *Bingamon*, 1928
         *Granco*, 1928
         *Trader*, 1923
22.    **Powell River**, floating breakwater saw a total of
         19 ships in line-up over an 80-year span, including:
         *Blatchford*, 1936
         HMCS *Coaticook*, 1953
         *Island Carrier*, 1945
         *Malahat*, 1945
         *Malaspina*, 1946
23.    **Oyster Bay**, 15 ships scuttled, including:
         HMCS *Charlottetown*, *Levis* and *Matane*, late 1940s
24.    **Kelsey Bay**, 6 ships scuttled, including:
         HMCS *Cape Breton*, *La Salle*, *Longueuil*
         and *Runnymede*, late 1940s
25.    **Royston**, 15 ships scuttled:
         *Black and Blue*, 1947
         *Crown Zellerbach #2*, 1962
         *Crown Zellerbach #3*, 1961
         *Forest Friend*, late 1950s
         HMCS *Dunver*, *Eastview*, *Gatineau*, and *Prince Rupert*, 1947-48
         *Laurel Whalen*, 1936
         *Melanope*, 1946
         *Nanoose* and *Qualicum*, 1946
         *Salvage King*, 1959
         *Tattnall*, 1947

Nootka Island

Bajo Point
5

Comox    ◐22    Powell River    ◄4
Royston    ◐25

*Strait of Georgia*

Newcastle Island

Union Bay

*Porlier Pass*

*Nookta
Sound*

Tofino

Port Alberni

*Burrard Inlet*

Ucluelet

Nanaimo    ◄18

6

*Barkley
Sound*

11 ◄

21 ◐◐  Vancouver
           Wreck Beach

◄17

Ladysmith

*Galiano Island*

Cape Beale

Victoria

*Kuper Island*

Cape Flattery

Esquimalt

*Puget Sound*

*Juan de Fuca Strait*

Port Angeles

Port Townsend

PACIFIC
OCEAN

Seattle

WASHINGTON

# Contents

The story that rivals those of the infamous *Flying Dutchman* all began when the *Maria J. Smith* wrecked off Barkley Sound in the late fall of 1869. After floating free of the rocks she had stranded on, the Downeaster was retrieved and then abandoned again, wandering the open ocean under full sail as a phantom ship before finally running aground on rocks off Aristazabal Island in Hecate Straits.

In January 1873, disturbing stories began to circulate of the fate of unverified survivors of the missing *Geo. S. Wright*. Wildly speculative reports that passengers from the vanished American steamer had been massacred or enslaved by a fierce tribe of Canadian Indians arose such controversy that the shipwreck soon took on the stature of an international incident.

On the night of April 29, 1883, the *Grappler* was in Discovery Passage and about four miles south of Seymour Narrows when a fire caused crew and passengers to abandon ship. Survivor John McAllister told the *Daily British Colonist* that those who had abandoned the inferno helplessly watched the steamer ". . . going backwards and forwards . . . the passengers shrieking and yelling for assistance" as the flames spread.

The enthusiastic crowd that gathered at Rock Bay in Victoria's Inner Harbour on a spring evening in 1884 never imagined that the freshly built steamer they watched slip down the ways would one day be lying at the bottom of Jervis Inlet—or that rumours of sabotage would cling to the disaster. The deep, craggy bottom of Jervis Inlet keeps *Mermaid*'s final resting place a secret to this day.

Captain Davidson ordered the boats provisioned and lowered when the Cape Horn windjammer struck ground ". . . with a shock which shook her every plate." The *King David*'s company landed at Bajo Point on the rugged and inhospitable southwest corner of Nootka Island, where the shipwrecked sailors spent 33 wintry days in a hostile environment.

Known as a "witch of the waves," *Melanope* raced from Puget Sound, Washington, to Table Bay, Cape Town, South Africa, in an incredible 72 days. This record is doubly amazing because it was done short-handed after 18 of the 30-man crew mutinied and were put in irons by Captain Wills. Unfortunately, the iron ship was still some 3,000 miles from Cape Town, and now short-handed.

After *Capilano* sank five miles WSW of Harwood Island on October 1, 1915, the crew rowed easterly in search of land, eventually reaching Indian Point on the west end of Savary Island. They watched their ship slip beneath the waves and gave vivid descriptions of the steamship's demise; of how her lights remained ablaze as she sank and how, just before she went to the bottom, the steam whistle gave a final, solitary blast.

During the summer of 1918, "a vast fairyland of lights" was visible from the Point Ellice Bridge as the night shift of wartime shipbuilding was underway in Victoria Harbour. Beneath powerful searchlights the huge gantry derricks of the Foundation Company lifted their loads over a number of wooden ships in various stages of production. The names of the new vessels on the stocks left no doubt as to their intended purpose.

Hugh "Red" Garling, who sailed on *Laurel Whalen*'s sister ship, *Malahat*, was struck by the great expanse of deck—some 200 feet from fo'c'sle to poop—and the enormous flexing in her hull; the hogging and sagging as well as twisting, especially in a quartering sea. "In the fo'c'sle, or below, all about you was the dissonance of sounds her timbers made as they worked and resisted the flexing."

Able Seaman James Aird was dreading the trip to Triangle Island and had fears of impending disaster on what was to be his ship's last voyage. The crossing was one of the most dangerous stretches of water along the West Coast—Queen Charlotte Sound— and the weather was foul. Adding to his worries was the fact that many of the ship's complement were absent as a result of the Spanish flu.

There's always been talk about how it would have been possible, sometime in the past, for an Oriental vessel to sail or drift across the North Pacific to make landfall somewhere along our West Coast. When two actually completed this remarkable feat—one sailing into Victoria's busy harbour in 1922 and the other ending its arduous voyage in the remote Central Coast mill town of Ocean Falls in 1939—they caused quite a sensation.

# CHAPTER 12

On January 29, 1927, the big steam tug *Pacific Monarch* headed out from Masset Inlet, Queen Charlotte Islands, with the loaded log barge *Drumrock* on the towline. The tug was bucking into a southeast gale when Captain McLellan decided to turn around and head for shelter. With tug and barge safely in Takush Harbour, the deeply laden barge hung up on an uncharted rock and stranded.

# CHAPTER 13

*Bingamon* had only seen about three and a half years of barge service when, on July 7, 1928, she caught fire while anchored in Plumper Harbour, Nootka Sound. The *Victoria Daily Colonist* reported, "The log carrier *Bingamon*, now merely a shell with part of her stern levelled off, is being patched with canvas in the drydock for towing to the Fraser River . . ." Soon afterward, she was finally laid to rest on the mud flats off Wreck Beach.

"Better to be taken care of and wind up their affairs in gainful occupation than be transformed into scrap before their days of usefulness are done," remarked Harold Elworthy, manager of Island Tug & Barge Ltd., in April of 1937. Victoria's Inner Harbour towing firm had just bought the five-masted barquentine *Forest Friend*, which had been lying idle up the Fraser River since 1929, to cut down into a barge.

Adrift in a gale, Alan Heater drew his mouth organ out of his pocket and played *Home Sweet Home* to keep the crew's spirits up. Then, around 1:30 in the morning, a large object loomed out of the dark, which Captain Billington identified as Solander Island. Incredibly, *Dunsyre*, drifting stern first in the storm, rather than going up on the island or onto the rocks scattered throughout the water, passed through the passage unscathed.

Throughout the Second World War, Canadian industry undertook a massive shipbuilding program, actively immersed in building a substantial small-ship fighting force for the RCN. With the return of peace, the bulk of this wartime shipbuilding program (more than 350 fighting ships) was to be disposed of, but here on the West Coast a number of the larger vessels managed to find local peacetime employment.

Scattered just off the beach along the inside waters of British Columbia's southern coast are several collections of badly deteriorated and rusted remains of ship's hulls, used to build protective breakwaters. At Royston, directly across the bay from the town of Comox, there is one of the largest and most unusual of these hulk collections.

Archie McLaren couldn't sleep one particularly stormy night in September 1946—he was quite disturbed about the weather conditions as his ship, *Brig. Gen. M.G. Zalinski*, ran full speed ahead up Grenville Channel in BC's Inside Passage. Purser McLaren was so convinced that they were headed for a disaster that he woke up the ship's clerk to help him prepare to abandon ship if need be. His disturbing premonition held true.

## Contents

**CHAPTER 19**

As *North Sea* made its way across Milbanke Sound in the early evening of February 13, 1947, it was raining hard with a 30-knot southeaster blowing. As she turned into Seaforth Channel, the Ivory Island and then Idol Point lights were momentarily visible but then vanished from sight in the rainy haze. Travelling at full speed, the American cargo and passenger steamer slammed into Porter Reef and came to a stop with a crashing jolt.

**CHAPTER 20**

It was 1955 when Fred Rogers made his very first wreck dive on the steam tug *Point Grey*, which had struck a reef and sunk in the turbulent waters of Porlier Pass in 1949. The wreck, shuddering in the tide and appearing as if it might topple off the reef at any time, held Rogers in awe of its violent beauty. More than 50 years later, he defines this experience as, "The one that opened my eyes; we were now addicts for more adventure."

**CHAPTER 21**

Ask any old-timer down on the dock what he considers to be the most famous West Coast marine engine from the first half of the twentieth century and chances are he'll reply, "Easthope." Heavy-duty, slow-turning and easy to repair, Easthopes proved a natural fit for the hundreds of "misery stick"-propelled (powered by oars) fish boats. They also happened to be the first gasoline engine to be manufactured in Vancouver, BC.

# Introduction

West Coast Wrecks and Other Maritime Tales is a compilation of stories spanning some 140 years of British Columbia's maritime history, which I researched, assembled and was fortunate enough to see featured in such publications as the Victoria *Times Colonist Monitor*, *Western Mariner*, *The Beaver: Canada's History Magazine*, as well as in various Underwater Archaeological Society of BC shipwreck reports over the past 20 years. Most of the chapters are tales of shipwrecks, but the book goes beyond just relating the circumstances that led to many a good ship going to the bottom. In one chapter, for instance, I explain how a number of retired Cape Horn windjammers gained a new lease on life as coastal barges and then, when they were worn out, ended up scuttled as hulks for a logging company breakwater. In another I set out to solve a 60-year-old mystery: How did Wreck Beach earn its name?

I also investigate the history behind the most famous early marine engine in British Columbia, the Easthope, but more importantly, throughout the book I allow some unique coastal characters to step forward and tell their stories. There are old towboaters such as Joe Quilty and Alan Heater, who risked their lives as a matter of course, along with a short biography of the King of West Coast Shipwrecks himself, retired diver Fred Rogers.

So what set off this interest and obsession with West Coast maritime history many years ago? While I did come from a family with a seafaring background (Dad served in the Royal Canadian Navy for 21 years), it wasn't until I began exploring Comox Logging & Railway Company's old hulk breakwater at Royston, just south of Courtenay on Vancouver Island, that I really became hooked on old ships and their fascinating stories.

I first explored the Royston site in the early 1970s, back when the 15 derelict ships scuttled there were still reasonably solid and standing proud off the beach, but it wasn't until I moved to the Comox Valley permanently, in the mid-1980s, that I began asking questions about the unusual collection.

Since there were obviously the remains of two or three nineteenth-century windjammers, along with a number of steam tugs and warships, scuttled seaward of the logging company's booming ground, I was confident that someone must know the identity of them all. Not so, I soon discovered. After talking with a number of long-time residents and making a diligent attempt to locate old company records, I was shocked to find that very little was known about the graveyard. Luckily, I came across some articles by BC history writer T.W. Paterson, who had already investigated the site, that appeared in Victoria's *Daily Colonist* and *Crown Zellerbach News* in the early 1970s that set me off in the right direction.

Finally, in 1992, after a lot of old-fashioned detective work that allowed me to confirm and build on Paterson's findings, I submitted a story on the site to the *Resolution: Journal of the Maritime Museum of*

*British Columbia*. Once it was published, it was full steam ahead tackling other facets of our coastal maritime history.

My next serious undertaking was working up the story behind all the retired sailing ships that had been cut down into barges by BC towboat companies in the 1920s and 1930s to transport logs, sawdust and hog fuel along the West Coast. Of course, I was ecstatic when my story was featured in the Victoria *Times Colonist* (see Chapter 14) but then, a few days later, a letter arrived in the mail. The first line read: "As one writer to another I have taken the liberty of amending the odd phrase or construction in your article." I was crestfallen; I had put so much into the story, and yet had still gotten a couple of details wrong. Of course, the letter was written by someone who knew his stuff; Bent Sivertz had sailed on one of the ships, the five-masted barquentine *Forest Friend*, as a teenage deckhand back in 1922–23.

Looking back, I recall that incident with fondness as it introduced me to a fascinating old salt whom I would otherwise never have met. It was the start of a great friendship, one I learned a lot from, and in the end that short letter was far more rewarding than the cheque I received from the newspaper.

Inspired, I went on to write other stories and eventually connected with the Underwater Archaeological Society of BC in the mid-1990s. At that time, then president Jacques Marc encouraged me to join the association even though I wasn't—and have yet to become—a diver. The UASBC is perhaps the most active and dedicated group of volunteer underwater archaeologists in North America and it has made an enormous contribution to the documentation and recording of shipwrecks along Canada's West Coast.

Still, the most rewarding aspect of exploring maritime history for me has been the opportunity to meet and interview countless individuals who lived and worked BC's challenging West Coast waters. Whether they were deepwater sailors who travelled the sea lanes of the world or those who spent most of their lives on inside waters towing booms from upcoast camps to south coast lumber mills, all have fascinating stories and adventures to relate.

Inevitably, *West Coast Wrecks and Other Maritime Tales* includes some stories of disaster at sea in which lives were lost. I hope this book, therefore, will serve as a written memorial to all whose bones lie on the bottom along one of the most treacherous stretches of coastline anywhere on the planet.

## Acknowledgments

I won't attempt to list all those who provided support with all my research and writing endeavours and were there to answer my never-ending stream of phone calls and emails with research queries, but some stand out from the rest; people such as Leonard McCann, Curator Emeritus at Vancouver Maritime Museum, and Eric Lawson, who informed me back in the early 1990s that my first big project, setting out to document the historic ships of Royston's hulk breakwater, was indeed a very important undertaking. As it happens, Eric knows his stuff, having spent time in the Falkland Islands, the graveyard of ships wrecked rounding Cape Horn and whose beaches are littered with windjammers and steamers dating as far back as the early nineteenth century.

Of course, whenever I started on a shipwreck story, the first person I'd get on the phone to would be none other than Mr. West Coast Shipwrecks himself, Fred Rogers. Frank Clapp, too, who maintains impeccable records on the innumerable vessels that worked our coast, deserves special mention for always being there to answer a tough question; and then there was Captain Harold D. Huycke Jr. on whom I relied as the expert on Cape Horn windjammers on the Coast.

I still don't think I could really have made a go of it if were it not for some great editors such as Ross Smith, editor of the Maritime Museum of BC's journal *Resolution*, and Peter Salmon, editor of the Victoria

*Times Colonist Monitor* back in the 1990s. Also, I can't say enough about Rob Morris and publisher David Rahn, of *Western Mariner*, with whom I have maintained a great relationship for some 20 years now. Then, of course, there are Jacques Marc and David Stone, who always made sure I got things right once I was hooked up with the Underwater Archaeological Society of BC.

The diligent staff and volunteers of the excellent archives and museums we're fortunate enough to have here on our coast also deserve special mention. Particularly hard-working and knowledgeable are those with the Maritime Museum of BC and British Columbia Records and Archives Service in Victoria, CFB Esquimalt Naval and Military Museum, the Vancouver Maritime Museum, the Puget Sound Maritime Historical Society in Seattle and the J. Porter Shaw Library in San Francisco, along with the National Archives and Records Administration in both San Francisco and Seattle. For any records I needed access to in Ottawa, there was No. 1 researcher Ken McLeod, ever willing to lend a hand.

Still, were it not for my partner and in-house editor, author Paula Wild, I don't know if I would have even set out on this voyage in the first place. Her key to becoming a successful writer? "Don't keep talking about it, just do it!"

Bow of the *Riversdale* at Royston, BC. RICK JAMES PHOTO

# Chapter 1

# *Maria J. Smith*:
# The *Flying Dutchman* of the
# West Coast, 1869

On November 14, 1869, Victoria's *Daily British Colonist* reported that "the schooner *Surprise*, Captain Francis, arrived from the West Coast Vancouver Island yesterday morning having on board Captain David Smith of American bark *Maria J. Smith*, his wife and children and officers and crew. The bark was wrecked on Tuesday morning last near Barkley Sound. All hands escaped to the shore and the second was left in charge of the wreck."

Only some seven years old at the time of her loss, the three-masted barque *Maria J. Smith* (named for his wife) was the ship of Captain Smith's dreams. Smith's father was claimed to be the richest man in Chatham, Massachusetts, and the family invested their money in shipping and maritime interests. Although David Smith was a carpenter and a schoolteacher through the 1850s, he also owned a business that canned and hermetically sealed seafood provisions. He made a whaling voyage to the Pacific and Arctic Oceans and, by 1859, was captain of the trading schooner *Mary E. Smith* running commercial freight between Philadelphia, Pennsylvania, and Mobile, Alabama.

In 1862, master mariner Smith signed a contract for $21,000 with Toby & Littlefield, shipbuilders located in Portsmouth, New Hampshire, for the construction of *Maria J. Smith*, a 475-ton wood vessel built out of eastern oak. She was to measure 113 feet long and 28 feet in breadth. Noted in Smith's logbook were instructions for the forward cabin to be painted, the after cabin to be finished in hardwood, and ". . . a house for the accommodation of crew and galley" to be built upon the main deck. While Smith was the majority shareholder, Toby & Littlefield agreed to take a one-quarter interest, with a number of other individuals retaining smaller shares in the barque. By the time the vessel was equipped and ready for sea, $34,000 had been invested by the shareholders.

*Maria J. Smith's* maiden voyage in the fall of 1862 was from New York to Montevideo, Uruguay, carrying assorted cargo and passengers along with Smith's wife and their three young daughters. A year later, records from the Shipping Master's Office in New South Wales, Australia, indicate that *Maria J. Smith* ". . . of Boston, David Smith, Master, Burthen 494 tons . . ." arrived in Sydney in distress from Newcastle on November 14, 1863. Along with the ten crew members aboard (two had died at sea) there were three passengers—Smith's wife, one of his daughters and a Miss Armstrong. The following year, Mrs. Smith succumbed to cholera on a voyage to Burma.

Over the next seven years, the barque made long voyages to ports all over the globe, reportedly with excellent returns. In two years alone during the Civil War, Captain Smith was said to have earned $70,000 as his share with *Maria J. Smith*. In 1865, the *Smith* made a voyage from New York to Europe the long way around—via Australia, China and the East Indies. The barque returned to the West Coast in 1868 with a cargo bound for Seattle but while being towed into port a violent storm sprang up. The tug was forced to cut the towline and the *Maria J. Smith* consequently ended up on the rocks. Unfortunately, the insurance on the vessel had been allowed to lapse. Upset with the disaster, Smith refused to return home until he repaid the loss to family and friends who were the vessel's shareholders. It would take him nine years to fulfil his promise.

Once repaired, the ship received a charter for a voyage from San Francisco to the Chincha Islands. Located 10 nautical miles off the coast of Peru, these dry and desolate islands were a major centre of a nineteenth-century shipping boom. It was the discovery of massive deposits of accumulated seabird feces—in hills over 100 feet high—that led to a guano rush. The bird droppings' particular balance of nitrates, phosphates and potassium made this the ideal fertilizer for replenishing the depleted soils of Europe and the United States.

An entry in the Captain's account book, dated September 4, 1869, noted that although the vessel was still in debt, this voyage to the Chinchas proved particularly lucrative and helped put Smith back on the road to solvency. Unfortunately, in early November 1869, *Maria J. Smith* was to find herself in distress once again.

The lumber-laden barque sailed from Port Townsend, Washington Territory, on the evening of Saturday November 6, 1869, passed Cape Flattery light at 2:00 p.m. on November 8, and by 6:00 p.m. was fighting a strong gale with a high sea running from the south-southeast when the deck load of lumber began to work itself loose. Soon afterward the vessel started to leak and then, with the wind steadily increasing, some of her sails were carried away. Once the blow began to ease up, topsails were hoisted in an effort to get away from land sighted close by, but this effort proved futile.

Captain Smith, who arrived in Victoria with his family and crew aboard the schooner *Surprise* on November 13, 1869, after being rescued, gave a report to the *British Colonist* as to what happened next. "(We) got the best boat out, and when nearly in the surf, got all hands into her safely and left the ship to her fate . . . Not knowing on what part of the coast we were, we laid by our boat waiting for daylight, which came at last and revealed to our sight one of the most terrific views imaginable: the sea was running mountains high and breaking over the reefs with irresistible fury . . . With much difficulty and no little damage we found our way among the rocks and breakers . . .

"At this time we were visited by a white man, Peter Francis, a trader, and found we were ashore at the extreme entrance of Barkley Sound, Vancouver Island. He informed us he had a house nearby and invited us all to take provisions and make ourselves as comfortable as possible. We accepted his invitation with many thanks and were heartily glad to find a warm fire and lunch awaiting. On Tuesday, Wednesday and Thursday we employed our time in saving what we could from the wreck and trying to get her afloat again, but the Indians were very numerous and troublesome, stealing everything that came to hand . . . On Friday there was a very high tide and the wreck floated off which we succeeded in getting to anchor in a small harbour where Mr. Francis' trading post is, since which time the Indians have ceased to steal, and by threats of sending a man-of-war to punish them have got some of the stolen goods back again . . ."

This anonymous Chinese painting of the *Maria J. Smith* in a typhoon is from George Francis Dow's *The Sailing Ships of New England*, Series Three (1922), plate #687.

According to *Lewis & Dryden's Marine History of the Pacific Northwest*, the *Maria J. Smith* was apparently written off as a wreck, since she was sold to "Broderick" for $950, her lumber for $750 and the sails for $300. (This was probably Richard Broderick, a coal and shipping agent and wharf manager in Victoria.) On December 21, 1869, the *British Colonist* reported that the American steamer *Politkofsky*, Captain Guindon, had left for the scene of the loss to retrieve and then tow *Maria J. Smith* to Meigs Mill, Port Madison, Washington Territory. Here she was to be discharged, docked and repaired. ". . . Her damages are slight."

Although *Politkofsky* managed to tow the wrecked barque clear of Barkley Sound, they encountered a severe gale once they were out in the open Pacific and were forced to cast *Maria J. Smith* free. According to the *British Colonist* of January 5, 1870, ". . . after the blow the steamer lost sight of her. *Maria J. Smith* had a crew on board, and there is just the remotest room for the indulgence of the hope that she will reach San Francisco." Captain Smith and his crew were on the barque at the time, while his wife (probably his second) and children remained safely behind in Victoria.

Five days later, an unidentified (probably Washington Territory) newspaper went into more detail on the failed salvage attempt. "At 9 o'clock on the morning of Dec. 31st, steamer started with the bark—weather moderate—but found, on arriving . . . a heavy southwest sea running. At 2 p.m., parted the hawser; ran up the bark's lee; passed out another hawser, and bent it on the other, started ahead again. At 8 o'clock, it began to blow fresh from the eastward, increased until 11 o'clock, making a nasty cross sea; found it impossible to steer the steamer with the bark in tow, and was obliged to let her go for our own

The steamer *Politkofsky* was built in New Archangel (today's Sitka, Alaska) in 1863 by the Russian-American Company. She was never a "gunboat" as some accounts suggest but was employed as a harbour tug and used primarily for towing sailing vessels in and out of Sitka Sound. BAINBRIDGE ISLAND HISTORICAL MUSEUM, IMAGE #336

safety. She was heading south by east when last seen, and behaved as well as any vessel loaded with lumber that leaves the Sound, answering her wheel with charm . . . We are informed that the bark *Maria J. Smith* was in good sailing condition, with plenty of sails and provisions and five men on board, and there is not the . . . danger of her going ashore or making a harbour short of S.F . . ." Still, the *Port Townsend Weekly Message* of January 7 did note that, ". . . the vessel was in a very critical condition when left being full of water, having knocked a large hole in her bottom while lying on the rocks . . ."

Then, on the 14th of the month, the steamer *Politkofsky* arrived in Victoria with a Mr. G.A. Meigs (owner of Meigs Mill, Port Madison, as well as of the steamer *Politkofsky*) and Captain Smith of *Maria J. Smith* aboard. In giving his account of what had transpired after they were cut free from the steamer, Smith reported that they beat about for 12 days trying to enter the Straits but, owing to the waterlogged state of the barque, were unable to do so. Thinking they were close to a lee shore, the Vancouver Island coast once again, Captain and crew abandoned the vessel for the second time and boarded a passing ship, the barque *Sampson*, on January 11. Then the wind changed direction. Once Smith learned from *Sampson*'s captain that they were actually off Cape Flattery they took off in pursuit of the abandoned vessel. Unfortunately they were unable to overhaul her as she was some 10 miles to windward—with all sails set.

When it reported on the high seas drama, the *British Colonist* noted, "She is certainly a remarkable ship, and her adventures may yet fill a volume." Captain Smith remained hopeful since he was

The *Politkofsky* was later purchased by joint American and Canadian interests in 1868 and rebuilt in San Francisco. A year later, the "Polly," as she became known, was bought by George Meigs and William Gawley and was put to work towing log rafts and lumber vessels for their Port Madison, Washington Territory, lumber mill.
BAINBRIDGE ISLAND HISTORICAL MUSEUM, IMAGE #420

of the opinion that his ship was still afloat and could be rescued by a powerful tugboat. Still, it would be another two months before news was received of what had actually become of the phantom barque.

When the mail steamer on the run between Port Townsend and Alaska, the *Constantine*, arrived in Victoria from Sitka in mid-March 1870, the *British Colonist* reported that with her came news that the ". . . derelict bark *Maria J. Smith* has been found by Indians near Bella Bella and is now in the possession of Mr. Moss. [Probably Morris Moss, a well-known Jewish fur trader on the Central Coast.] The waif has sailed without aid of helmsman or compass nearly 500 miles from the point where she was abandoned, threading her way through intricate channels and dangerous tide rips to her present harbour of refuge. Twice this remarkable bark was abandoned and twice she has saved herself."

The *Olympia Washington Standard* reported that, "Capt. Small, of the steamer *Constantine*, informs us that on the 24th of February on the voyage from hence to Sitka, the steamer anchored at Fort Rupert near the north end of Vancouver Island and shortly after, a canoe arrived with Mr. Morse, the H.B.Co.'s Agent, who reported that the *Maria J. Smith* had drifted ashore on the west side of Aristazable [*sic*] Island just north of Milbanke Sound, and was hard and fast on a reef of rocks. Her cargo being of lumber will keep her from breaking up as fast as would have done if she had been empty or had been loaded with coal. She is a total loss. When last reported here, the bark had been seen off Cape Flattery. Since, she has drifted north some two hundred miles. The place where she lies is in Lat. 51 deg. 40 min. north, Long. 129 deg. 10 min. west."

The actual distance, as the crow flies, from Cape Flattery to Aristazabal Island, is about 375 miles—a remarkable feat indeed.

In 2003, while harvesting sea urchins, divers Pat Olsen and Rod Taylor located some anchor chain and other bits and pieces of wreckage off the west coast of Aristazabal Island. This information was passed on to the Underwater Archaeological Society of BC, a volunteer group of divers and underwater archaeologists, which was intrigued by the discovery since the society was in the midst of compiling its next report, the *Historic Shipwrecks of the Central Coast*. On June 8, 2005, some UASBC divers made a trip to the outer coast of Aristazabal Island to search for the wreckage. Unfortunately, after swimming more than a mile of coastline around the reported coordinates, nothing was found. The UASBC plans to return to the area sometime in the future and hopefully locate the remains of the ship of Captain David Smith's dreams, the barque *Maria J. Smith*.

# Chapter 2

# Steamship into Oblivion: The *Geo. S. Wright*, 1873

Weeks after the remains of a ship washed up on beaches near Cape Caution, Queen Charlotte Sound, in January 1873, disturbing stories began to circulate in US newspapers. Rumours had it that survivors from the missing American steamer *Geo. S. Wright* had been massacred by a fierce tribe of Canadian Indians. Worse yet, according to the wildly speculative reports, some of the female passengers had been captured and were being held as slaves. So much controversy arose in the newspapers of the day that the shipwreck soon took on the stature of an international incident.

At the time of the tragedy, *Geo. S. Wright* was operating under the flag of the Oregon Steamship Company and was on a return voyage to Portland after transporting mail, troops and supplies to Alaska. Twenty-one officers and crew along with about a dozen passengers were aboard when the *Wright* disappeared in late January 1873.

The screw steamer or "propeller" *Geo. S. Wright* was built for John T. Wright Jr., who named it in honour of his brother, and was launched in Port Ludlow, Washington Territory, on September 1, 1863. The wood steamer was schooner rigged with two masts and measured 118 feet long, with its steam machinery consisting of a single-cylinder engine that produced 125 nominal horsepower.

After *Geo. S. Wright* was launched for the Wrights' steamship fleet, she was soon making runs between Portland and Puget Sound with stops in at Victoria and New Westminster. Then, early in 1865, the propeller was bought by the Western Union Telegraph Company and spent the next two years involved with the company's enterprising Collins Overland Telegraph project. Western Union's goal was to extend a telegraph line north through the interior of British Columbia into the Yukon and then across Russian America (Alaska) and the shallow Bering Strait to link up with a telegraph line in Siberia. When completed, the ambitious project would connect the capitals of Europe with North America by telegraph. Unfortunately, the successful completion of Cyrus Field's underwater telegraph cable across the Atlantic in 1866 brought an abrupt end to the venture and it was officially suspended in February 1867.

Two years later, *Geo. S. Wright* was purchased by Oregonian Joseph Kamm and put back on the Portland, Puget Sound and Victoria run until the fall of 1869 when the ship was sold to the North Pacific Transportation Company. When Ben Holladay, President of the North Pacific Transportation Company of Portland, Oregon, purchased the *Wright* he was already recognized as the "Vanderbilt of the Pacific." Holladay managed to accumulate some 25 deep-sea steamers and, as maritime historian Norman Hacking noted, all except for one ". . . were purchased second-hand and were badly maintained . . . the lifesaving

Peter Rindlisbacher created this rendering of a possible scenario of the loss of the *Geo. S. Wright* off Cape Caution. PETER RINDLISBACHER

equipment was inadequate, and the navigational abilities of the officers were open to question." Between the years 1868 and 1870, four steamers from the Holladay fleet were lost to marine mishaps between Mexico and southern British Columbia.

Five steamers, one being *Geo. S. Wright,* in the North Pacific Transportation fleet were sold to the Oregon Steamship Company in August 1870. (The new steamship company was created by Ben Holladay in an attempt to avert a financial crisis.) At the time, several of the company's ships were employed transporting mail, troops and supplies to Alaska, which the United States had purchased from Russia only some three years earlier.

In early January 1873, *Geo. S. Wright* sailed from Portland, loaded coal at Nanaimo and headed north to Alaska on her final voyage. The steamer was commanded by Captain Thomas J. Ainsley, ". . . brother of a Mrs. Mouat of this city, an experienced pilot," according to Victoria's *Daily British Colonist.*

The paper also reported that on about the 13th of January the steamer stopped in at Fort Tongas where she took on freight, mail and passengers including John Williams. "Mr. Williams had $15,000 in gold dust in his possession." The *Wright* arrived in Sitka on the 19th and, after taking on more passengers and freight, departed two days later. In her final stop—at Kluvok—the steamer loaded a particularly heavy load of freight that was reported to be some 800 barrels of salmon and 100 barrels of oil, along with some skins and furs. In addition to her 21 officers and crew, it was estimated that *Geo. S. Wright* now had 11 or 12 passengers on board. On January 25, Captain Ainsley—possibly in a hurry to be home for his wedding to a Victoria woman—put to sea into a particularly bad snowstorm.

On February 27, 1873, Victoria's rival newspaper, *The Daily Standard*, broke the bad news with the headline: "Wreck of the Steamer *Geo. S. Wright*—probably Foundered at Sea." It was reported that when the steamers *Emma* and *Sir James Douglas* had arrived in Nanaimo the previous day with five Nuxalk (Bella Coola) canoes in tow, the natives had given a first-hand account of what they had come across two weeks earlier close to Cape Caution in Queen Charlotte Sound. The group reported that, while camping near the Cape, they discovered a large quantity of wreckage along the beach.

Among the items found were the deck of a steamer, the pilot or wheel house, parts of a mast, boxes, blankets, clothing and "the board bearing the name of the unfortunate vessel upon it . . ." and "having prosecuted a strict search for five days, gave up the hope for finding anybody, dead or alive, and hastened down to Nanaimo." As it happened, below the story on the wreck published in *The Daily Standard* was a letter from Alden Westly Huson, storekeeper in Alert Bay, who informed the paper that he had received news of the *Wright's* loss; somewhere near Cape Caution sometime earlier. Huson concluded with "I have no doubt but that all are past and gone."

In this engraving of the Western Union Telegraph Company Fleet, the square-rigged ship at centre is *Nightingale*, with the steam schooner *Geo. S. Wright* directly off her bow. Engineer-in-Chief of the project, Charles S. Bulkley, noted in a February 4, 1866, *New York Times* story that "...the steamer *George S. Wright* proved a valuable vessel, both economical and serviceable." Seven years later it was to be a different story. THE BANCROFT LIBRARY, UNIVERSITY OF CALIFORNIA, BERKELEY, BAN PIC 1950:004: 28.2

As it happened, a *British Colonist* reporter was able to learn more about the loss from his interview of the Central Coast Indians. He reported that they also came across ". . . a plank tied to a box as if some unfortunate on board a sinking vessel tried to make a raft . . ." and said that, not far from the beach in deep water, two masts were sticking out and that ". . . they could stand on the beach and toss a stone to the wreck."

When it reported the latest news on the marine tragedy the *Colonist* was quick to acknowledge ". . . that this brave little steamer has been lost, with all on board . . . and the cause may never be known." It continued, ". . . the steamer was very poorly provided with canvas, and that in the case of her machinery breaking down she would have much difficulty in sailing. When at Nanaimo the chief engineer wanted to have the ship beached to repair the discharge pipe; but for some reason this was not done. It is said, too, that he complained of his assistant (a new man) being incompetent. Other hands are said to have stated that the vessel was in very bad condition. Fierce gales prevailed on the coast during the month of January and it is thought that the disaster occurred on the downward trip, either by an explosion of the boiler (as in the case of the *Emily Harris*) or by the breakdown of the machinery." The *Victoria Standard* agreed, noting that the *Wright* had a broken escape pipe and that the "unfortunate" chief engineer, Mr. Sutton, had severe reservations about the voyage ahead. Overall, the *Geo. S. Wright* was ". . . in a very pitiable state to make any resistance to heavy gales, or to combat the terrific seas which are known to have prevailed in the locality of the disaster . . ."

It wasn't until early March that any kind of search vessel was able to steam north to the scene of the disaster. In Victoria, the United States consul pressured local authorities to dispatch the Royal Navy steam sloop HMS *Peterel* to search Queen Charlotte Sound. Across the border, concerned American citizens and distressed family members demanded that the USRC (United States Revenue Cutter) *Lincoln* be dispatched to the scene immediately. Unfortunately, USRC *Lincoln* met a heavy westerly swell entering Queen Charlotte Sound and turned back. According to the Collector of the Marine Revenue Service, M.S. Drew, the revenue cutter's boiler was defective and the ship was in no state to face the storm-tossed waters of Queen Charlotte Sound. Meanwhile, the *Wright*'s owners in Portland ordered North Pacific Transportation Company's sister ship on the Alaska run, *Gussie Telfair*, to leave immediately for the north.

HMS *Peterel* left Nanaimo around March 7 and on board were Captain Spaulding of the BC Provincial Police and James F. McGrath, owner of the Alert Bay store located on Cormorant Island, a small island off the northeast coast of Vancouver Island. McGrath was returning to the island to relieve his storekeeper, "Wes" Huson. By doing so, McGrath hoped Huson could join the warship as pilot and interpreter. He was very familiar with ". . . the habits of the Indians of Cape Caution," as well as being "intimately connected with the Captain and officers."

When *Peterel* rounded the corner into Alert Bay on its way north, British officers and crew were greeted with a disturbing scene; the Stars and Stripes was flying at the trading post. An offended Commander Cecil George Sloane Stanley RN was quick to bring McGrath, owner of the post, to task and reprimand him. In a letter to the *British Colonist* later that month, titled "That American Flag at Alert Bay," McGrath took great care to explain the background behind the perceived insult to Her Majesty's Government.

Apparently, Huson had raised the American flag at half mast hoping to draw the attention of the American steamer *Gussie Telfair* to have her stop in so he could convey news of the missing *Geo. S. Wright*. (As it happened, nailed farther down on the flagstaff, but not noticed until pointed out by McGrath, was the name board of the lost Oregon steamer retrieved at Cape Caution.) Still, Captain Stanley was not in the least impressed, especially since he may have been well aware that Wes Huson was an ex-Yankee from New York State. As a result, no invitation was forthcoming to the local trader to come aboard the warship and lend his assistance to the search.

This was a particularly unfortunate development. As one of the few whites in the District, Huson was probably more up on news of *Geo. S. Wright* than anyone else. Since there were only two trading posts in the area (the other was the Hudson's Bay Company's Fort Rupert), Alert Bay was a focal point for trade and supplies as well as a gathering place for the many tribes in the area. Indeed, when the steamer *California* stopped there three years later, it noted there were around "... some 400 Indians and one white man, Mr. West [sic] Huson."

On March 17 both HMS *Peterel* and Ben Holladay's steamer *Gussie Telfair* returned to Victoria with the sad news that neither a wreck nor any survivors from *Geo. S. Wright* were to be found.

The loss of *Geo. S. Wright* was reported in January 1873 but it was early March before any kind of search vessel was able to steam north to the scene of the disaster. The United States' consul in Victoria pressured local authorities to dispatch the Royal Navy steam sloop HMS *Peterel*, seen here, to search Queen Charlotte Sound. IMAGE FROM A LATE 19TH CENTURY EDITION OF *THE NAVY & ARMY ILLUSTRATED*

On instructions from the government, *Peterel* prosecuted a strict search along the coast. The Royal Navy sloop attempted to explore every cove and point, and fired guns and rockets day and night to alert survivors, while officers and crew in boats scoured beaches and reefs for clues. Still, *Peterel* was unable to land a search party anywhere near Cape Caution where most of the wreckage had been found. According to the *San Francisco Daily Evening Telegram* of March 19, 1873, "... Captain Stanley describes the coast as the roughest and wildest he in the whole course of his experience witnessed, and also pictures the neighbourhood of Cape Caution as a perfect pyramid of surf and waves."

Ben Holladay's *Gussie Telfair* sailed all the way to Alaska and back but, like the *Peterel*, was unable to land at Cape Caution. On its way down the coast, the steamer stopped at a number of villages to make inquiries. At Bella Bella, a trader named Lowden produced a barrel of oil he had purchased from some Indians, retrieved 200 miles north of Cape Caution. The trader bought the barrel along with an iron band torn from the mast as it lay on a beach. Natives also reported that on the beach near Cape Caution were signs of someone having built a house "... after the fashion of the white man." Regrettably, no one seemed to have any direct knowledge of the wreck or possible survivors.

In the end, according to the officers of the *Telfair*, *Geo. S. Wright* had probably struck the low sunken rocks of the Sea Otter Group a few miles outside Cape Caution. In response to this report on the loss, an "Old Salt" wrote the *British Colonist* to point out that after he learned how much freight the steamer had taken on in Kluvok alone, he'd come to the conclusion that the *Wright* was terribly overloaded. "May she not have been too deeply laden for any emergency likely to arise in the winter season ... had her decks been swept by a heavy sea, filled and gone down?"

Writing to the *Colonist* on March 23, James McGarth noted that he had it on good account, that the Aurkeno (probably Oweekeno, who occupy the head of Rivers Inlet) Indians were the first on site at the wreck of *Geo. S. Wright*, "... on their way down to the Fanaughtas [?] to a feast." They picked up valuable furs by the bale. "One Indian is said to have picked up 100 sea otter skins. The Indians are *mum* about anyone getting ashore." McGrath reported that, the week before, he had been told that two white men actually got ashore where the skins were found. Still, "The Indians are laughing how they fooled the man-of-war again. It is a pity the Awikenos [*sic*] were not visited. It is too late now."

In a letter to Wes Huson on March 22, McGrath was somewhat more forthcoming with details than he was in his letter to the *Colonist*. "The *Telfair* did not call or did anyone see her; Ben Holladay had better look sharp. Some of those pilots might cause the Cooper dodge on him [probably James Cooper, Dominion Agent for Department of Marine and Fisheries]. It is strange too she might not have called at Nanaimo. Now I don't know if she will proceed to the wreck. It will be forgotten now as the first ex-citement was frustrated. I am of the opinion that it was done intentionally to turn the *Lincoln* back for fear she would proceed to Owikeno and get a loop hole on those Indians. The matter ought not to be dropped in the District. Old Spaulding [Captain, BC Provincial Police Force] is smart . . ."

When someone with the pen name "Suwanee" wrote to the *Puget Sound Daily Courier* in late March claiming they'd heard two men and a woman reached the shore from the wreck of the *Wright* and were seized by the natives, the men eaten, and ". . . the woman kept for vile purposes," readers of the *British Colonist* were incensed. What was particularly gal-ling was that the "brute" charged that these horrific deeds were a direct result of "the teachings and ad-vice of the British authorities" who taught natives to abhor Boston Men (i.e. Americans; the British were called King George Men.) "We really think that the alacrity with which the Canadian government sent a British war-ship in the vicinity of the wreck, and the zeal with which the officers of the ship prosecut-ed their search, should have protected our people from the publication of charges which only a vile mind could conceive . . ."

Residents of Victoria had good reason to be annoyed. While the *Geo. S. Wright* was indeed fly-ing under the Stars and Stripes and was registered in San Francisco, many aboard on the fateful voy-age had close ties to Vancouver Island. Along with Captain Ainsley, who had a sister living in Victoria and was engaged to a young lady there, the chief en-gineer, John Sutton, had a large family in Victoria, as did his second engineer, James Minor. Purser Frank Weidler's brother was a steamship agent in the capital city, cook Jewell Michel's father lived in Esquimalt and passenger John Williams was

Alden Westly ("Wes") Huson, a storekeeper in Alert Bay and one of the few whites in the District, informed Victoria's *Daily British Colonist* in late January of 1873 that he had received news of the *Geo. S. Wright*'s loss somewhere near Cape Caution. *"I have no doubt but that all are past and gone."* HARBOUR PUBLISHING COLLECTION

formerly of the Victoria firm, Evans & Williams. (The paper didn't bother to report what village the three native crewmen hailed from.)

Ironically, the editor of the *Courier* claimed that the Suwanee letters actually originated from an unnamed source in Alert Bay. (He pointed out that they were handed to him by a gentleman who ". . . is of the highest respectability" and who assured him that the writer was ". . . perfectly reliable and trustworthy.") Three days later, another letter to the editor appeared, this time from someone in Port Townsend who felt compelled to respond to the sensational story. "The letter in the COURIER of the 26th inst., from Alert Bay, signed 'Suwanee,' is all a fabrication. The same report was made to Capt. Stanley, of H.M. Steamship Petrel [*sic*], and he proceeded to the Indian mission [probably Harbledown Island] and interviewed the priest [probably Oblate Father Leon Fouquet], from whom the rumour was said to have started, and the whole thing is pronounced false. There is no ground for the report. It is a falsehood, cut from whole cloth, and should be denounced immediately."

With the return of HMS *Peterel* and *Gussie Telfair* to port later in March, reports of wreckage and bodies found slowly drifted in from up coast. On March 27, the steamer *Otter* returned to Victoria with a boy's copper-tipped shoe and a life preserver. The Indians from whom Captain Lewis retrieved these items also related that they had found the body of a boy, ". . . a *sitkum* or half-breed and aged about eight years . . . the body had been frightfully mangled by dogfish. Even the little shoe bears marks of the voracity of these fish." The body was discovered in Hykin (Hiekish) Narrows, Finlayson Canal, and it was believed to be that of Charles Waldron's son. The fact that the small body was wearing a life jacket indicated that those aboard had had enough time to prepare themselves for whatever had befallen the ship. (It was suggested at first that the boiler might have exploded, which would never have allowed those aboard the opportunity to escape, let alone don a life jacket.) The *Otter* also learned that Captain Ainsley probably changed his mind and chose to come down through exposed outside waters rather than staying within the sheltered Inside Passage. Ainsley was to blow the steamer's whistle when passing Bella Bella, signalling to residents there that he was safely on his way south. No one ever heard it.

By April, Ben Holladay had promised to spend $150,000 to launch a search for relics from *Geo. S. Wright* and her crew and passengers since he felt some might still be alive. Earlier that month, two Tsimshian canoes that had stopped at Alert Bay had reported that the body of a man, which the group buried, had been found in Indian Cove at Cape Caution. They were also fortunate enough to recover several packages of skins.

When the sloop *Yellow Lane* returned to Victoria from Skeenamouth on April 26, it reported that they had put in at Indian Cove (a safe anchorage at Cape Caution) on the way south where wreckage of *Geo. S. Wright* lay on the beach. The party on board found the foremast, bowsprit, part of the wheel and some cabin planking. While the mast was intact with no damage, ". . . the bowsprit was shivered [splintered] as if it had struck a rock." Those on the sloop also learned that another body was discovered some distance north at Aristazabal Island. The partial remains were those of a man lashed to two chairs with a wool comforter and wearing a life jacket while some cabin furniture and planking were found washed ashore. Another month was to pass before any more relics surfaced.

In late May, the gunboat HMS *Boxer* left Esquimalt with the Superintendent of Indian Affairs, Dr. Powell, aboard to interview tribes of the north. On stopping in at Bella Bella, a keg, a lantern, a candle, a fragment of a newspaper and some biscuit were obtained, supposedly off *Geo. S. Wright*. On the way south *Boxer* stopped in at Takush Harbour, Smith Sound, where the natives were found ". . . to be both well disposed and quite in contradistinction [*sic*] to the letters written by 'Suwanee.'" They also reported that

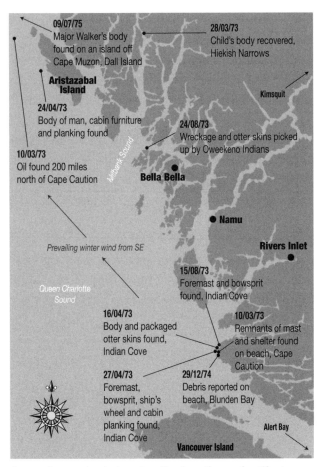

A wreckage chart showing the locations of artifacts and bodies recovered from the lost American steamer *Geo. S. Wright*. The actual location of the wreck site or who was behind the massacre of survivors—if there indeed was one—remain shrouded in mystery. BASED ON A MAP CREATED BY JACQUES MARC

they had no tidings of the wreck. When the sloop *Duncan* arrived in Victoria on June 23 Captain Collins produced more relics—a cigar holder, a meerschaum pipe and part of an account book—which he said he had purchased from Indians some 175 miles north of Cape Caution.

On August 2 the Portland *Oregonian* reported that, ". . . earnest efforts have been made at Portland to elicit interest enough to induce the dispatch of a vessel . . ." to try to determine what became of the 32 people aboard the lost *Geo. S. Wright*. Among those who were "unremitting and indefatigable" in their requests to have a steamer sent out on a search were Mrs. A.B. Sutton, wife of the engineer John Sutton. On April 19, 1873, Mrs. Sutton forwarded to the Secretary of the Treasury a petition signed by a number of prominent Oregon citizens appealing to the government to send out a vessel at once to look for the *Wright*. Letters were also written to the President of the United States, Ulysses S. Grant. (Oregon descendants of the *Wright's* engineer, John Sutton, state that family lore has it Sutton attended West Point with Ulysses S. Grant.)

However, it wasn't until early August 1873 that an American government vessel, USRC *Lincoln*, arrived on the scene in Queen Charlotte Sound. Since the lifeboats from *Geo. S. Wright* were yet to be found (in the end, they never were) it was speculated that survivors might be living on the beach somewhere along the coast. Captain A.B. Davis stressed that no pains were spared by the cutter's crew and officers in their attempts to locate anyone still alive. After an intensive search throughout Queen Charlotte and Milbanke Sounds, all that was found were some skins and a copper plate from the *Wright's* gangway, which was obtained from Nuxalk natives when the *Lincoln* stopped in at Bella Coola.

"These Indians were found to be peaceable and quiet, and according to the Hudson's Bay Company living among them . . . all stories of foul play are utterly without foundation," noted Captain Davis. He finished his report to US government authorities by noting that the ". . . the rumors and reports of foul play being done to any of the passengers and crew of the 'Wright' were instigated by a few unreliable and unprincipled white men, whose reputation in British Columbia is very bad."

The missing *Geo. S. Wright* was slowly fading into memory as just another one of a number of shipwrecks along the North West Coast in the mid-nineteenth century, when, two years later, natives reported seeing a makeshift European-style shelter on a rocky coast. Then, in July 1875, the body of John Stevens Walker, Major, United States Army, who had boarded the *Wright* in Sitka, was found on the beach at Bazan Bay, Dall Island, off Prince of Wales Island, Alaska. Part of his skeleton was found in the remains of his dark blue Army of the Union uniform and greatcoat, all held together by a lifejacket. The discovery was destined to be the final chapter in the tragic tale of *Geo. S. Wright*; that is, until a year and half later.

In early 1877, Bella Bella Chief Charley Hemsett related a peculiar and disturbing story to Alfred Dudower, a high-ranking Tsimshian and captain of the trading schooner *Ringleader*. Hemsett said he met a native named Billy Coma, living in Nanaimo, who claimed to be the coal passer on *Geo. S. Wright* when she wrecked. According to Coma, after the steamer was swamped by mountainous seas in January 1873, he, along with 14 other survivors, struggled onto two small islands somewhere off Cape Caution. That night, their fires attracted some Oweekeno canoes whose occupants landed and set upon the hapless group, robbing them and slitting their throats. Fortunately for Coma, who was a Nimpkish (a 'Namgis native, one of the many Kwakwaka'wakw Nations), he was able to claim an Oweekeno blood connection that saved him from certain death.

When these startling new revelations were brought before the authorities, Lieutenant Charles Reynold Harris, in command of the gun vessel HMS *Rocket*, was ordered to steam north from Esquimalt in March 1877. Also aboard the warship were Sergeant Bloomfield of the Victoria police, representing the civil authority, and George Hunt, an interpreter, who was picked up in Fort Rupert. Once in Central Coast waters, landing parties were sent ashore at various villages to perform interrogations and obtain scraps of information from various First Nations.

On March 30, 1877, HMS *Rocket* arrived off the Nuxalk village of Kimsquit in Dean Channel. Here a series of events led to a terrible outcome. Sergeant Bloomfield of the BC Police was sent ashore with a small party to demand that the Kimsquit chiefs hand over four individuals implicated in the massacre. Only two suspects were delivered up and, after a fight broke out on the beach when one of the chiefs refused to cooperate, the chiefs were warned that the village would be destroyed if the other two suspects were not brought to the ship.

When the pair weren't forthcoming, Harris put the ship in a position where the *Rocket*'s guns could be levelled on the village. He then ordered the villagers to stand clear as the settlement was fired on and set ablaze in reprisal. The residents could only watch as their homes and possessions were destroyed.

"The settlement, which had probably numbered one hundred or more before the shelling, was uninhabitable and was abandoned, and its population dispersed to other settlements," wrote maritime

---

### Last Voyage of *George S. Wright*

**21 Officers and crew:**
Captain Thomas J. Ainsley; B.F. "Frank" Weidler, purser; and John Sutton, chief engineer—all of Portland;
James Minor, second engineer;
Daniel Noonan, first officer;
William Price, second officer;
P. Clawson, Owen McGough, firemen;
Edward Johnson, Archibald Dunn, James Irwin, Gus Proffe, J. Jensen, seamen;
Chris Adams, steward;
Pedro Salvo, Jewell Michels, cooks;
C. Hevendehl, waiter;
Moses Baptiste, pantryman;
Indian James, messboy;
Indian Jack and Jim, coal-passers.

**11 or 12 Passengers (sources are contradictory):**
Major John Stevens Walker, Paymaster, US Army, and his wife;
Lieutenant Henry C. Dodge;
Charles Waldron;
Charles Kincaid;
Mr. Sincheimer; a former cooper from the Kluvok fish saltery;
John Williams;
a "Frenchman" returning from the Omineca gold fields;
a miner on the Stikine River;
Mr. Hogan and son.

historian Barry Gough in *Gunboat Frontier: British Maritime Authority and Northwest Coast Indians, 1846–1890*. Gough went on to say that the unfortunate incident was ". . . among one of the last cases of sanctioned use of violence by the Royal Navy . . . to teach recalcitrant natives that crimes against Whites and property would be repaid in kind."

Four native people—two Oweekeno and two Nuxalmc (Nuxalk people) from the village of Kimsquit—were arrested, taken to Victoria and charged, but later that year, when the matter came up in court, it became clear that a grave mistake had been made. Referring to the Crown's star witness, the *British Colonist* reported on October 20, 1877, that "the Indian reported as being saved from the wreck is said to be one who served a long term in the Victoria jail." In his final statement before His Honour, H.C. Courtney, the Superintendent of Police told the court that the lone witness to testify against the four accused was ". . . an Indian named Coma . . . bearing so bad a character that it is almost impossible to believe him." The Superintendent stressed that the Attorney General had done all he possibly could but was still unable to

In March 1877, the gun vessel HMS *Rocket* arrived off the Nuxalk village of Kimsquit in Dean Channel with Lieutenant Charles Reynold Harris (centre, sitting on a chair) in command. Sergeant Bloomfield of the BC Police (at left, leaning on the rail) was sent ashore with a small party to demand that the Kimsquit chiefs hand over four individuals implicated in a massacre, setting off a series of events that led to a terrible outcome. COURTESY OF ROYAL BC MUSEUM, BC ARCHIVES A-00255

come up with any evidence at all to corroborate Coma's statements. Consequently, all charges were dropped and the prisoners discharged from custody. On hearing the outcome, a Captain Thomas Laughton told a reporter that he wasn't at all surprised, adding that he was certain Coma was not on board *Geo. S. Wright* at the time and ". . . that if anyone ought to be punished it certainly should be Coma."

Today, over 130 years later, the actual details of the loss of the *Geo. S. Wright,* the location of the wreck site or who was behind the massacre of survivors—if indeed there was one—remain shrouded in mystery. As noted in *Lewis & Dryden's Marine History of the Pacific Northwest,* ". . . all that can be said is that she sailed away and no message ever came to quiet the heartaches of those whose friends and relatives perished with her."

**Final footnote:**
Even before the trial was over, Ben Holladay's European bondholders had already caught up with him. He lost his fleet of steamships early in 1876, his over-extended transportation empire collapsed and the "Vanderbilt of the Pacific" died in Portland in July 1877. In July 2009, the Underwater Archaeological Society of BC, as part of its survey of Central Coast shipwrecks, anchored off Indian Cove at Cape Caution and did an underwater as well as a beach survey of Indian Cove and Blunden Bay hoping to locate remains of the lost steamer. The group came up empty-handed.

# Chapter 3

# Gunboat Grief:
# The Loss of the *Grappler*, 1883

Twenty-four-year-old Lieutenant Edmund Hope Verney arrived in Esquimalt from England in May 1862 to assume command of his new ship, HMS *Grappler*, a combination sail and steam gunboat. The young Verney soon discovered that the three-masted, 108-foot-long, shallow-draft vessel (the gunboat only displaced 6.5 feet) was a pleasure to handle under sail. Two years later it was a different story. After rigorous service along the Northwest Pacific coast, Verney began to complain that *Grappler* had become defective, steamed badly and that her bottom was "all knocked about."

The Commander-in-Chief of the Pacific Squadron eventually paid heed to these dismal reports and the gunboat was put on the market in the fall of 1867. It was while going about her business as a commercial freighter after passing into private hands that the *Grappler* was involved in one of the worst marine disasters on the West Coast.

Lieutenant Verney's predecessor, A.H.P. Helby, had left HMS *Grappler* in excellent condition and in the hands of a well-disciplined crew with a positive attitude back in the spring of 1862. Crew and officers deserved to be proud: their warship was one of a new design to join the Royal Navy (RN) fleet. The idea of the gunboat as a purpose-built ship for the RN had come about as a result of the need for a revised naval strategy during the Crimean War (1854–56.) The reluctance of the Imperial Russian forces to battle the British and French navies confined allied operations to blockading and attacking enemy coastlines, and this new reality soon highlighted the value of steam over sail.

Nearly 100 of the Albacore class, like *Grappler*, were built, but haste in constructing them resulted in the use of unseasoned timber and many of the vessels later fell to pieces. As is happened, not one was completed in time for active service in the Crimean War, but both HMS *Grappler* and her sister ship HMS *Forward* did take part in the St. George's Day naval review held by Queen Victoria at Spithead to celebrate the end of that war.

Following the Fraser River gold strike in 1858, the Admiralty dispatched a number of warships to the colonies of Vancouver Island and British Columbia to secure British sovereignty and maintain law and order. HMS *Grappler* and HMS *Forward* sailed from England in August 1859 after being specially fitted out for their new role. While the United States government would use its army to quell disturbances throughout its frontier West, Great Britain had its own answer for unruliness along the fringes of its vast empire: send in a gunboat.

It was hoped that the mobile, shallow-draught vessels would not only offer the means to counter

In the fall of 1862 *Grappler* transported a number of settlers to Comox, BC, pioneers of what was soon to be a thriving agricultural community. BILL MAXIMICK PAINTING

Indian threats but, more importantly, would act as a presence to forestall any American territorial ambitions imported with the hordes of American forty-niners flooding the Fraser River gold bars. Once the gunboats reached Esquimalt in July 1860, they were quickly discovered to be ideally suited for the treacherous and restricted coastal waters of the Northwest coast.

Although *Grappler* was often preoccupied with more mundane activities—laying navigation buoys in the Fraser River, serving as a lighthouse tender, aiding ships in distress—the ship did take part in some noteworthy historic events. During the summer and fall of 1862, the *Grappler* transported a number of white settlers to both the Cowichan and Comox valleys on Vancouver Island, pioneers who subsequently founded these areas' first agricultural communities.

The sister ships HMS *Forward* and *Grappler* also played central roles in the Lemalchi incident in the spring of 1863, when the gunboats were used to hunt down the Indian murderers of some Gulf Island settlers. In the attempt to bring the perpetrators to justice, the Kuper Island village of the Lemalchi people was levelled by the guns of *Forward*.

After another two years of hard service, and Lieut. Verney's growing concern over her condition, the overworked *Grappler* was paid off on May 13, 1865. A Captain Frain purchased her for $2,400 in 1868 and, soon after passing into private hands, the clean-hulled profile of the Royal Navy gunboat was altered by the addition of an ungainly midship house. The silhouette of the warship-steamer conversion was to remain a familiar figure in coastal waters for 15 years—up until the night of her loss on April 29, 1883.

In May 1862, 24-year-old Lieutenant Edmund Hope Verney arrived in Esquimalt from England to assume command of his new ship, HMS *Grappler*, a combination sail and steam gunboat. He soon discovered the vessel to be a pleasure to handle under sail. COURTESY OF ROYAL BC MUSEUM, BC ARCHIVES I-51693

An April 1883 advertisement in the *Victoria Daily British Colonist* announced that the steamer was to depart for Fort Wrangel (today's Wrangell, Alaska), Skeena and Rivers Inlet from the Dickson, Campbell & Co. wharf at 6:00 p.m. on April 28. The coaster left that evening headed up the coast with a cargo of cannery supplies and around 100 passengers, most of whom were Chinese cannery workers. The following day *Grappler* stopped at Nanaimo for 40 tons of coal, discharged 50 kegs of powder and immediately left. The steam schooner *Grace* was hailed that afternoon and a pilot was taken on board.

At 9:55 p.m. on the night of April 29, when the *Grappler* was in Discovery Passage and about four miles south of Seymour Narrows, a fire was discovered behind her boiler by engineer William Steele. The donkey engine was immediately started and a hose connected, but once it was realized how serious the blaze was, the crew and passengers ran for the boats to abandon ship. The inquiry that followed learned that Captain John Jagers ordered the pilot to head the ship for the Vancouver (probably Vancouver Island) shore.

Unfortunately, the steamer became unmanageable once the fire had burned through the hemp ropes connecting the wheel to the rudder. To complicate matters, due to the heat, no one could get near the engine room to slow the vessel down, so the ship was still travelling at full speed. The *Grappler* continued to run out of control for some time, constantly changing course from one side of the channel to the other.

The vessel came equipped with only two lifeboats but cannery owner John McAllister had shipped four fishing skiffs of his own. He went to clear the boats but found it next to impossible to lower them properly. Both the smoke from the blaze forward and McAllister's inability to communicate with his panicking Chinese employees complicated any attempt to get the boats into the water in an orderly fashion. One turned bottom up but at least one was successfully launched. Of the steamer's two lifeboats, one of them made it into the water right side up and picked up several survivors from the water.

A few of the many who jumped overboard found themselves immersed in the frigid waters of Discovery Passage clinging to bits of flotsam tossed overboard by crew and passengers.

John McAllister, who pulled himself into one of his skiffs after jumping over the side, told the *Daily British Colonist* that those who had abandoned the inferno helplessly watched the steamer ". . . going backwards and forwards . . . the passengers shrieking and yelling for assistance" as the flames spread.

The newspapers of the day provided the names of the 21 white survivors while noting that "two Indians" and "13 Chinamen" were also saved. Captain Jagers, who stayed with his ship as long as possible before being driven off by the flames, was among those found alive. Estimates of those who perished that night varied from 70 to as high as 90. The exact number of lives lost remains unknown since the purser's records were lost with the ship.

On May 5, 1883, the *Daily British Colonist* reported that on the morning following the catastrophe the ill-fated steamer was last seen drifting down from Seymour Narrows with the tide and that she finally ". . . sank beneath the waves in 30 fathoms of water at the same spot she became unmanageable." The sleek gunboat of which Lieut. Verney had assumed command in the spring of 1862 had met a tragic end as a fiery wreck 21 years later.

An inquest was held in Victoria into the death of Donald McPhail, passenger on the *Grappler*, and on May 15 the jurors found that the SS *Grappler* was not licensed to carry passengers on leaving the port of Victoria on April 28 and did so without making provisions for their safety. They also declared the owners (Warren and Saunders of Victoria) and officers of culpable negligence.

*Grappler* is in the foreground in this photograph of the Royal Navy Fleet at Esquimalt, BC. The mobile and shallow-draft gunboat was ideally suited to her new role in Pacific Northwest waters. VANCOUVER MARITIME MUSEUM #2772

Captain Jagers' reputation appears to have survived the consequences of the inquiry. Once he had recovered from his horrendous experience that fateful night, he was given charge of the steamer *Beaver*. He was later employed by the Canadian Pacific Navigation Company where he commanded a variety of well-known coastal steamers.

Steele, one of the most prominent marine engineers in British Columbia in the nineteenth century, also survived the disaster. The ill-fated *Grappler*'s chief engineer went on to take charge of the government dredge employed in Victoria Harbour and on the Fraser River and remained with that service as superintendent until his death in 1893.

In 1868 the former Royal Navy gunboat *Grappler* passed into private hands and her sleek lines were marred by the addition of a square midship house, seen in this photograph taken in Victoria, BC. COURTESY OF ROYAL BC MUSEUM, BC ARCHIVES G-06346

# Chapter 4

# On the Bottom of Jervis Inlet:
# The Paddlewheeler *Mermaid*, 1904

The enthusiastic crowd that gathered at Rock Bay in Victoria's Inner Harbour on May 31, 1884, never imagined that the freshly built steamer they watched slip down the ways that spring evening would one day be lying on the bottom of Jervis Inlet—or that rumours of sabotage would cling to the disaster.

A Victoria *Daily Colonist* reporter, who witnessed the launching, reported that the new side-paddle wheeler *Mermaid*, ". . . was gaily decorated with English, American and other flags, and the launch was achieved in a perfectly successful manner." The reporter then went on say that *Mermaid*, ". . . was intended for towing purposes and her model and build are highly creditable to her experienced builder."

The wooden steamer—74 feet in length, 18 feet wide, 5.25 feet in depth and fitted with two high-pressure steam engines producing 26 combined horsepower—was built to order by H.B. Bolton of Victoria for a partnership of four individuals with connections to Hastings Mill in Burrard Inlet. Partners Richard H. Alexander (sawmill manager), Mary G. Raymur (wife of former manager Captain R.A. Raymur), Ainslie J. Mouat (accountant) and Charles A. Coldwell (sawmill foreman) intended to use the *Mermaid* as a towboat and general workboat.

Hastings Mill was built in 1865 on the southern shore of Burrard Inlet where the National Harbour Board is now located in the Port of Vancouver. It was one of the first major lumber export mills established in British Columbia. Historic photographs of the site taken in the late nineteenth century often feature large sailing ships tied alongside the sawmill's dock loading lumber while others lay anchored out in the stream waiting their turn. Steam tugs were required for towing the windjammers into and out of the harbour and berthing them, as well as for other general sawmill duties. By 1896 Hastings Mill was operating a fleet of around eight towboats.

*Mermaid* worked—apparently uneventfully—for Hastings Mills for around nine years, and was then sold to the Northern Shipping Company Ltd. of Vancouver on March 14, 1893. The new owners replaced the paddlewheels with twin screws and her high pressure engines with two new steeple compound steam engines.

It was only a matter of months before the steamer was in trouble. Northern Shipping was attempting to run *Mermaid* as a coasting steamer serving the ports of Victoria and Nanaimo with stops throughout the Gulf Islands when she lost a propeller in Ganges Harbour on December 22, 1893.

Captain John W. Gisholm managed to return the steamer to Nanaimo on one engine but her troubles weren't over, as Northern Shipping Company was already undergoing financial difficulties. The company had been in the hands of a liquidator since October and, on June 2, 1894, he ordered Northern Shipping's business affairs wound up. *Mermaid* was consequently sold to the New Vancouver Coal Mining & Land Company, Limited (NVCM&L).

NVCM&L was a British firm that had taken over the original Hudson's Bay Company land grant and coal interests in and around what is today's town of Nanaimo, BC. One of their mines, the Protection Mine, was under Protection Island, a small island off the Nanaimo waterfront. The coal mining company was soon using *Mermaid* both as a tug for towing barges and a ferry to carry miners across the water from their Nanaimo homes to Protection Island.

*Mermaid* went on the rocks in Kanaka Bay, Newcastle Island, on March 12, 1902, and NVCM&L decided to sell the stranded steamer as is, where is. Charles Wardill, a steam engineer, purchased the vessel, made temporary patches to her bottom and had her towed to Victoria for repairs.

Wardill was originally hired by the NVCM&L soon after his arrival in Canada from England. He worked in the shops of the coal mining operation and acted as a steam engineer for the company's locomotives and tug. Judge Stanley Wardill (Charles' grandson in Nanaimo) recalled that after his grandfather bought *Mermaid* he attempted to run the vessel as a steam packet to carry loggers and supplies from Vancouver into Jervis Inlet. Stan Wardill heard from other family members that his grandfather sank everything he had into the venture and probably didn't bother with insurance on the steamer, which was valued at $22,000 in turn-of-the-century dollars.

In the early morning darkness of March 25, 1904, *Mermaid* was running at full speed in Jervis Inlet with Mate Roberts at the wheel and a crew of six and three passengers aboard. Charles Wardill, who was acting as chief engineer, had brought three of his children along: Stan's father Mike, who later ran a bicycle shop in Nanaimo; Oz, who went on to become a Nanaimo schoolteacher; and Kate, who eventually married and moved to California.

The *Mermaid* had just dropped off some loggers in Vancouver Bay when, at 5:00 a.m., she turned the corner too soon, struck the rocks of Moorsam Bluffs and stove in her bows. Captain Walters attempted to run his sinking ship across Jervis Inlet to beach it on the Brittain River flats several miles away but the rising water flooded the boiler room forcing Chief Engineer Wardill to abandon his post, and the vessel consequently lost steam and came to a stop. The lifeboat was launched while the captain and engineer stayed aboard for as long as possible in an attempt to save the holed vessel.

Although it was only a short distance to shore, *Mermaid* sank in 60 to 100 fathoms of water. The crew and passengers spent the next

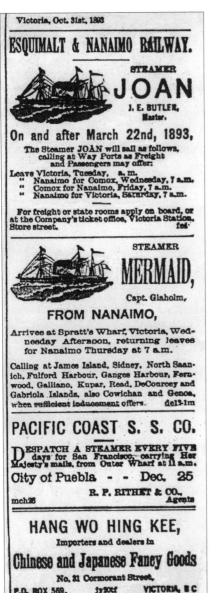

This advertisement for the Victoria-Nanaimo passage of the steamer *Mermaid* appeared in the *British Colonist* newspaper in 1893.

UNDERWATER ARCHAEOLOGICAL SOCIETY OF BRITISH COLUMBIA COLLECTION

The *Mermaid* was employed towing barges and ferrying miners from Nanaimo, BC, to a mine on nearby Protection Island when she stranded on the rocks at Kanaka Bay, Newcastle Island, in March 1902. NANAIMO MUSEUM COLLECTION Q3.89

two days rowing the lifeboat out to Pender Harbour where they were able to catch Union Steamship's *Comox* for Vancouver, where the press was informed of the disaster.

To this day the tale persists among the Wardill family that someone had been intentionally put aboard *Mermaid* to sabotage her and put an end to Charles Wardill's challenge to Union Steamship's monopoly of the run. Some even say he had been warned in particular to watch out for her captain.

The Underwater Archaeological Society of BC tried using side-scan sonar in May 2001 to locate the remains of *Mermaid,* but the attempt was unsuccessful. The deep, craggy bottom of Jervis Inlet keeps *Mermaid's* final resting place a secret to this day.

# Chapter 5

# The *King David*:
# Did Lost Crew Join Doomed Ship?
# 1905

On April 5, 1973, Comox Valley residents witnessed a peculiar sight: a Canadian Forces Labrador helicopter passing overhead with a large anchor dangling beneath it. The unusual artifact was once an essential part of the ground tackle of *King David*, a three-masted steel sailing ship wrecked on Bajo Reef off the west coast of Vancouver Island in December 1905.

The three-masted British ship *King David* (pictured here in about 1900) was in ballast and in-bound for Royal Roads, Vancouver Island, when—in the midst of a southwesterly gale—she drove ashore on Bajo Reef, Nootka Island. STATE LIBRARY OF SOUTH AUSTRALIA PRG1373/15/57

Someone had happened to notice the anchor in the intertidal area of Santa Gertrudis cove in Nootka Sound and had convinced the 442 Transport and Rescue squadron at Canadian Forces Base Comox it was worth recovering for the Courtenay and District Museum. Its heart-shaped palms and square shank indicated that it was a nineteenth-century Admiralty pattern anchor, probably forged in the 1840s in Great Britain for a sailing ship. What wasn't known at the time was that the owner of a log salvage business, who was also a diver, had deposited the anchor and a capstan from the *King David* wreck site at the convenient location after recovering them from Bajo Reef.

The 2,240-gross-ton, 279-foot-long British ship *King David*, owned by the Glasgow Shipping Company, left Salinas Cruz, Mexico, in ballast for Royal Roads, Vancouver Island, on September 30, 1905. According to the January 20, 1906, edition of the *Victoria Daily Colonist* the vessel was 74 days out and on the overdue list when she finally drove ashore on Bajo Reef. Although the survivors reported it a slow voyage, the trip had gone reasonably well until *King David* approached Vancouver Island. There a series of southwesterly gales and snow squalls carried the vessel to the north.

She arrived off Nootka Sound on December 10 in calm conditions only to face another gale that night. The anchors were let go to hold the big windjammer off the beach but they dragged bottom three days later and huge seas drove *King David* onto the submerged rocks of Bajo Reef. (The *Colonist* reporter located Bajo Reef by noting that it stretched seaward south of Bajo Point two miles north of Maquinna Point "where the great whale totem and the weather-broken sewing machines and rusted rifles mark the grave of Chief Maquinna.")

After the Cape Horn windjammer struck ". . . with a shock which shook her every plate," Captain Davidson ordered the boats provisioned and lowered. Experiencing the massive steel hull breaking up on the rocks apparently unhinged the old sailmaker, Donald McLeod, who became deranged and had to be forcibly restrained in one of the boats. The ship's company landed at Bajo Point, the rugged and inhospitable southwest corner of Nootka Island, to encounter rocky cliffs open to the Pacific and then dense forests and impenetrable salal undergrowth inland. The shipwrecked sailors spent 33 wintry days in this hostile environment.

The stranded seamen had only limited knowledge of the local area and were unaware that they were only about eight miles away from Friendly Cove. The village had a number of Indian lodges and also a well-stocked general store that contained more than enough provisions to feed 25 shipwreck survivors. The captain sent two men out to reconnoitre and, within two days, they met a wandering prospector, but unfortunately his knowledge of the area was as vague as their own. He told them—incorrectly as it happened—that a steamer wouldn't be by until March.

Oblivious to the fact that they were so close to rescue, Captain Davidson sent his ship's boat off with his chief officer, A. Wallstron, and six men to Cape Beale, a lighthouse some distance to the south. As

**JANUARY 20, 1906.**

# King David Is a Wreck

**Eighteen Survivors Are Rescued From Bajo Point by Queen City.**

**Chief Officer and Six Men Who Went for Assistance Believed Drowned.**

**Shipwrecked Men on the Beach for Over a Month —Sailmaker Dead.**

In the *Victoria Daily Colonist*, dated January 20, 1906, a crewmember of the *King David* reported that the doomed voyage "went along fairly well until we got off the Vancouver Island coast, and then we struck a series of southerly and southwesterly hail and snow squalls." UNDERWATER ARCHAEOLOGICAL SOCIETY OF BRITISH COLUMBIA COLLECTION

The *King David*'s Chief Officer, A. Wallstron, and the six men who were sent out in a ship's boat to find help at the Cape Beale lighthouse may have been picked up by the in-bound, four-masted steel barque *Pass of Melfort* (pictured here around 1898). Unfortunately, the barque herself wrecked off Ucluelet, BC, with loss of all life. STATE LIBRARY OF SOUTH AUSTRALIA PRG1373/17/36

Davidson explained later, when he first made landfall he was disoriented because he had old charts and had mistaken a new light at Clayoquot for Cape Beale. Wallstron and the other six seamen and the boat were never seen again.

The *Daily Colonist* suggested that the small boat's course probably crossed that of the ill-fated *Pass of Melfort* inbound in ballast from Panama for Port Townsend, Washington. The four-masted barque was itself caught in a southeast gale and wrecked on Amphitrite Point at the entrance to Ucluelet Harbour. There were no survivors to say whether their ship had indeed picked up the seven *King David* sailors.

The 18 men who remained huddled under tarpaulins and canvas at their barren campsite on Nootka Island were ultimately more fortunate. When they had spent more than a month on the inhospitable shore, the vessel *Queen City* noticed their fire and rescued them. The ordeal was too much for the old sailmaker, however, and he died aboard *Queen City*.

Today, the big anchor in the Comox Marina parking lot sits unrecognized as once belonging to *King David*, a stately Cape Horn windjammer that met its end off the West Coast with the loss of eight lives. To many who pass by the anchor, it's just another of the numerous bits and pieces recovered from the ocean floor that are often found decorating parks and the yards of sport divers.

### A final note

Underwater archaeologists suggest that interesting artifacts found on the ocean floor are better off left where they are. Most objects submerged in salt water reach an equilibrium point where deterioration stops due to a lack of oxygen, but once out of the water, the artifacts often quickly turn into an unrecognizable pile of rust. Another point to remember is that the British Columbia Heritage Conservation Act clearly states that it is against the law "to damage or alter a heritage wreck or remove any heritage object from a heritage wreck" without an authorized permit.

Passersby can't help but notice the massive early 19th century Admiralty pattern anchor on display in the Comox Marina parking lot but most are unaware that it once belonged to the *King David*, which met its end off the West Coast in 1905 with the loss of eight lives. RICK JAMES PHOTO

# Chapter 6

# *Melanope*:
# Witch of the Waves, 1905

Launched from the shipyard of W.H. Potter & Company in Liverpool, England, in 1876, the iron three-masted *Melanope* was the subject of curious tales in her day. For most of her life she was considered a cursed ship, while others who sailed the vessel actually found her a pleasure to sail and a "witch of the waves." One of her last masters, Leighton Robinson, recalled in later life how it had been to handle *Melanope*. "She was very fine aft with a clean run and fine entry forward, never lost steerage way during my experience with her, and an able vessel in heavy weather."

While nearly all of the hulks at Comox Logging & Railway Company's abandoned breakwater at Royston on Vancouver Island have long since collapsed into the estuary mud, there is one whose bow section was still holding up in the spring of 2011—the old Cape Horn windjammer *Melanope*.

In 1966, Bruce Watson recounted to *Vancouver Sun* marine writer Charles Defieux his impressions of rowing around the breakwater hulks as a boy. Particularly fascinated with *Melanope,* he would peer through a hole in the waterline. "I could lean inside and view in the musty interior the changing patterns of light produced by sun-rays poking through the rotting planking and open mid-section. The exposed ribs were webbed with strings of seaweed beaded with water droplets and the light glistened from these, the rusty spikes, the rippling water of the flooded area, and the dripping water from the fallen beams. It was an eerie and haunting sight."

*Melanope* was one of the thousands of square-rigged iron and steel windjammers that flourished across the oceans of the world in the late nineteenth century. Although these massive, slab-sided, flat-bottomed vessels lacked the fine lines and elegance of their forebear, the wooden clipper, they were often almost as swift. Still, many considered them no less attractive than their wood ancestor since the ornamentation of the hull and deck fittings, often teak, was just as lavish.

In essence, these tall ships symbolized the last gallant attempt of the age of sail to challenge the arrival of the steamship. They earned the name "windjammers" because their crews were required to "jam" or brace their yards all the way around in order to get the monsters to sail into the wind. Still, whereas a clipper ship often required a crew of 35 to 40 men, the new windjammers were usually managed with about 30. However, the iron ships did suffer from some shortcomings, especially since owners and builders were reluctant to reduce the top hamper—the overall weight of the rigging—and had a tendency to over-mast the ships.

As a three-masted ship 258 feet long and of 1,686 gross tons, *Melanope* was rigged with a standard

Before leaving San Francisco for Australia in 1900, *Melanope* (pictured here riding at anchor off Sydney, Australia) was "rigged as a barque and poorly rigged in the way of running gear at that," according to her new captain, Leighton Robinson. PUGET SOUND MARITIME HISTORICAL SOCIETY #1587

rig of the day and carried double top-gallant and royal sails above her upper and lower topsails and mainsails. The huge mainsails of a typical windjammer often weighed a ton dry and considerably more when wet. The iron yards (the spars from which the sails are set), sometimes 90 feet in length and 2 feet in diameter at the centre, were in themselves extremely heavy. When the miles of wire rope, chain and manila line needed to support this collection of masts, sails and yards were added, the weight aloft became terrific. Even though wire backstays were doubled, the strain on the rigging was still enormous. *Melanope* herself suffered the consequences from an overly generous sail plan on her first voyage.

The ship was constructed for a prominent rice milling and trading firm—Heap & Sons of Liverpool, England, and Rangoon, Burma. They maintained a fleet of six or seven ships carrying cargo and emigrants from Great Britain outward to Australia and bringing goods from Southeast Asia to European ports on the return trip.

Marine writer Basil Lubbock once told a curious tale concerning *Melanope*'s maiden voyage, and almost every writer since has made a point of including the story in their own account of the ship's exploits. It appears that as *Melanope* was being towed out of the Mersey River to open water, an elderly woman selling apples was discovered on board. The ship's master, Walter Watson, was quick to act and had his potential stowaway deposited onto the towboat headed back to port. The indignant lady left in a huff, cursing both the ship and all aboard as she went. Of course, every mishap that was to befall *Melanope* from that day onward was attributed to this unpleasant incident.

The premonitions of an already superstitious crew appeared vindicated when their new ship got into trouble only a few days out from Liverpool. On October 7, 1876, *Lloyd's List* reported that *Melanope* had returned to Canning Dock, Liverpool, after being dismasted some 200 miles northwest of Cape Finisterre in a gale. The underwriters who inspected the vessel tried to convince the crew that the mishap was directly attributable to the shipbuilders having over-masted the iron ship by nine feet.

After repairs were made, *Melanope* set sail for Melbourne, Australia, and over the next few years the ship carried new immigrants out to Australia and then loaded rice or jute in Southeast Asia for her return voyage to Great Britain. In 1882 the Heap & Sons fleet was sold to William Gracie and Edwin Beazley of Gracie, Beazley & Co., who subsequently formed the Australasian Shipping Company that same year.

Sailing ships continued to earn good dividends for their owners by transporting three great bulk cargoes throughout the 1880s. The Calcutta, Rangoon and Chittagong jute and rice trades, the San Francisco and Puget Sound grain trade and the Australian wool trade were all booming at this time. In essence, the huge iron and steel square-riggers were the forerunners of today's container ships; floating storage bins used to transport the raw materials in high demand by Europe's new industrial age. For outbound voyages, the windjammers loaded cotton, heavy machinery, rails, coal or salt. As a result, the Australasian Shipping Company was able to keep *Melanope* fully engaged as a merchant ship throughout the 1880s and 1890s.

As the 1890s progressed, *Melanope* became more involved with charter work along the Pacific coast of the Americas. By December 1898, *Melanope* was found sitting at a dock at Antwerp, Belgium, and it was here that Basil Lubbock picked up his "cursed ship" tale once again. This time the supposedly ill-fated ship was bought by a disreputable master. Captain J.R. Craigen was apparently a ". . . very thirsty master mariner, who had run off with the equally thirsty and very rich daughter of a wealthy Indian officer." When the ship arrived in Panama in February 1900 and his bride succumbed to a fatal combination of drink and fever, it is said a broken-hearted Craigen put an end to his pain by jumping overboard. Fo'c'sle gossip had it that the mate assumed command, brought the vessel into San Francisco that summer and then quietly absconded with the dead captain's gold, leaving the crew "d.s." (distressed seamen).

*Melanope* was seized and sold by a United States Marshal on November 27, 1900, for $53,900 to an American citizen. The new owner offered young Leighton Robinson the command and he accepted on the condition that he could take his new bride with him. Writing in 1930, Robinson remarked, "I took charge of her here in 'Frisco in the later part of 1900 leaving the *Coptic* and took Kate with me on voyage to Sydney, Australia. She was then rigged as a barque and poorly rigged in the way of running gear at that. Pope and Talbot owned her . . . they wanted a man with British licence to take command. She had come up from Panama with scrap iron, part of the old French Canal stuff. J.J. Moore of the Australian Dispatch Line were agents [a San Francisco lumber exporting firm]."

Unlike the earlier honeymoon trip, the Robinsons' passage to Sydney, Australia, with a cargo of lumber aboard was trouble free and completed in a record time of 45 days. Captain Robinson considered Lubbock's story of *Melanope* in *Last of the Windjammers* as "a lot of bunk . . . particularly that pertaining to the purchase at Antwerp etc." Before taking on his charge, Robinson made a point of questioning one of the crew about the incident. "The story I got from Green, who was mate, was that the captain Creighton [*sic*] and his wife, who was a Miss Emma Taylor, had purchased the vessel at Antwerp, intending to cruise around the world. On reaching Panama she died of fever, and he didn't care whether he lived or not, and contracted fever of which he died en route to S.F. There were a lot of newspaper write-ups etc. and all sorts of weird yarns about his having other wives and running away with the lady who purchased the vessel for him, but I don't put much stock in any of that."

The iron square-rigger set a record in 1903 that probably has yet to be equalled by a vessel under sail. During August and September, the iron ship shifted between the lumber mill towns of Port Townsend, Port Ludlow and Port Blakely, Washington State. On September 10 *Melanope* was finally under sail and passing out past Tatoosh Island. Known as a "witch of the waves," the iron ship raced from Puget Sound, Washington, to Table Bay, Cape Town, South Africa, in an incredible 72 days. This record is doubly amazing because it was done short-handed after 18 of the 30-man crew mutinied.

Captain Wills was dissatisfied with the way the helmsman had allowed the ship to drift off course and, after the crewman denied it, put him in irons for insolence. When some of the crew protested the severity of this punishment, Wills—armed with a revolver and his mates with clubs—called them one by one up to the poop. Each member who refused duty was then put in irons as well. Unfortunately, *Melanope* was still some 3,000 miles from Cape Town, and now short-handed.

N.K. Wills, who retired in Vancouver, BC, told a reporter for the city's *Province* newspaper in 1942, "Oh, she could pass anything under sail . . . . We handled her alright. We had fair winds and we all knew our business." When they reached South Africa on November 23, 1903, the mutineers were tried and sentenced to work in a rock quarry for six weeks until the ship cleared for Newcastle, Australia, on January 8, 1904. Although there was no trouble from the malcontents on this voyage, they were dismissed in Australia and signed off with no reason given on their papers. This action by the captain was tantamount to beaching them.

After filling her holds with coal in Union Bay on Vancouver Island in early 1906, *Melanope* sailed for Unalaska in the Aleutian Islands in the spring. Upon returning to the Pacific Northwest, she then set sail from Bellingham, Washington, to Manzanillo with a cargo of railroad ties aboard and, before she reached there, was caught in a hurricane off the Mexican coast. Once she was in safely at the port and had delivered her cargo, *Melanope* left Manzanillo on November 1 on what was to be her last voyage.

The wrecked barque *Melanope* was towed into Astoria by the steam schooner *Northland* in December 1906. After encountering a violent storm off Cape Blanco, Oregon, the ballast in the *Melanope* had shifted and she had gone over on her beam ends, forcing crew and passengers to seek refuge in the rigging. SAN FRANCISCO MARITIME NHP, E3,2.304

Charles Wills, son of Captain Wills and nine years old at the time, recalled the details of the loss of *Melanope* to maritime historian Norman Hacking in 1975. She was sailing north on her way to Tacoma, Washington, with sand ballast in her holds when she ran into a violent storm off Cape Blanco. The ballast shifted, the mainmast was dislodged, and the ship went over on her beam ends. In an attempt to save her, the fore and main topmasts were cut away, with the main topmast and royal yards toppling through the main topgallant stays and rigging before they crashed through the deck. Captain Wills, his wife, son and daughter and the crew of 22 were forced to spend a harrowing night in the rigging and it was not until morning that they were able to clear a lifeboat from the half-submerged deck.

Fortunately, they were found and picked up by the steam schooner *William H. Smith* and taken to Port Townsend, Washington. *Melanope* herself was discovered later as a drifting derelict with a severe starboard list off the Oregon coast. The steam schooner *Northland* put a line aboard and towed her into Astoria on December 14, 1906. Three days later, the Wills family were reunited with their dog, Queenie, who had been left behind on the wreck.

As *Melanope* was damaged beyond repair, J.J. Moore & Company sold the 30-year-old windjammer. She was bought by James Griffiths, an entrepreneur in Puget Sound marine transportation, who had made a good part of his fortune by purchasing retired sailing ships and turning them into barges. The tall ships were shorn of rigging and had their hatchways enlarged, while some also had their main deck torn out.

James Griffiths & Sons also owned and operated a Canadian subsidiary, the Coastwise Steamship and Barge Company of Vancouver, BC, with eight vessels, all registered as barges and all built between 1872 and 1885. The stripped-down three-master was put into service between Puget Sound, Northern British Columbia and Alaska for Griffiths' Coastwise Steamship and Barge fleet. Among other jobs, *Melanope* probably barged rock from Waldron Island, in the San Juan Islands, to Grays Harbor where a jetty was being constructed.

On May 25, 1911, James Griffiths sold *Melanope* to the Canadian Pacific Railway (CPR) who bought her to replace their old collier, *Robert Kerr,* which had wrecked in the Gulf Islands that March. *Melanope* remained a familiar sight around the West Coast for decades, but still it was distressing to see what was once a majestic tall ship now weather-beaten and looking forlorn at the end of a towline as a coal hulk. "It was like discovering the armless and legless trunk of a once-beautiful statue," William McFee, a former mate on a tramp steamer and author of *The Watch Below,* reflected while bunkering his ship from another square-rigger turned collier. "The ship's bowsprit had been sawn off flush with the stem, her masts were cut down . . . . She was black with coal dust and crusted with grimy sea salt."

The collier *Melanope* worked on a regular run from the Union Bay and Ladysmith loading facilities on Vancouver Island to the CPR docks in Burrard Inlet for some 30 years. Although now only a weather-beaten coal barge, *Melanope* remained a source of peculiar tales. R.E. Griffin recalled striking up a conversation with an old sailor while looking over the hulk. The sailor enlarged on the story of the curse and told Griffin that when the mizzen mast was removed, 32 pounds of opium were found stashed inside it.

The blackened collier was seen regularly in Burrard Inlet waiting to bunker the graceful white ocean liners *Empress of Russia* and *Empress of Asia.* The big liners were requisitioned as troop transports

In her reincarnation as a collier, *Melanope* is seen here rafted next to the CPR's trans-Pacific liner *Empress of Asia* in Burrard Inlet, BC, discharging coal. CHARLES BRADBURY PHOTO, 1916, COURTESY OF ROYAL BC MUSEUM, BC ARCHIVES A-07162

While the hulls of the ships surrounding her have all collapsed into the estuary mud, the bow and stern section of the *Melanope* still remain standing at Royston. The steel hull plates of the CPR tug *Qualicum* and HMCS *Dunver* are now only piles of rusted wreckage while the wrought iron construction of *Melanope* still maintains the structural integrity of her remaining elements—a proud testament to British shipbuilding at the height of the Victorian age. RICK JAMES PHOTO, 2011

during the Second World War and, unfortunately, both were lost. The *Asia* was turned into a fiery wreck off Sumatra by Japanese bombers in February 1942 while the *Russia* was destroyed by fire during an overhaul at Barrow-in-Furness, England, in September 1945. This effectively brought *Melanope*'s career as a coal hulk to an end. Although she also supplied some coal to the CPR's tugs and galley coal to the "*Princesses*" of the company's British Columbia Coast Service, the CPR deemed her no longer essential in 1946.

"Old *Melanope* To End Days As a Breakwater," the *Vancouver News Herald* announced on April 12, 1946. The *Vancouver Province* of the same day stated: "Proudest, fastest full-rigged sailing ship afloat in her heyday, *Melanope* will be sunk in shallow water off the Comox Logging & Railway Co. wharf at Royston." Retired Captain N.K. Wills came down to have a last look at his old command before she left Burrard Inlet on the towline. He was very interested to discover that the bird's-eye maple was still intact on the bulkheads of his quarters, while his bath—close to four feet deep—could still hold water.

*Melanope*'s registry was finally closed with the note, "Vessel beached & broken up . . ." and she was left to the mercy of the weather and sea at Royston. By the early 1950s, the southeasterlies had collapsed her bulwarks, leaving only her bow and stern sections intact. Local residents were happy to discover that the old collier still had some cargo in her hold and that preparing for the cool winter months was only a matter of picking up coal washed up on the beach.

At the time of writing, although the hulls of the other 13 vessels that were scuttled at Royston have nearly all completely disintegrated, the wrought iron plates of *Melanope* still hold her bow high—some 135 years after her launching at the height of the Victorian Age when Britannia still ruled the waves.

# Chapter 7

# Loss of the Union Steamship
# *Capilano*, 1915

On October 4, 1915, a small news item appeared in the *Vancouver Sun* titled, "Crew Brings News of Disaster." The paper reported that, "according to the word brought by the crew of the Union Steamship company's steamer, *Capilano*, which sank on Friday night at a point midway between Savary Island and Cape Mudge, the vessel struck . . . some obstruction some eight hours before disaster and

The single screw steamer *Capilano* was the second of three steel ships built in Scotland for the Union Steamship Company of British Columbia Ltd., which was formed to transport passengers and cargo around the BC coast.

although an examination was made of the hull when the boat put into Van Anda [on Texada Island] . . . she sank shortly after leaving that port."

The single screw steamer *Capilano* was the second of three steel ships (the other two were *Comox* and *Coquitlam*) ordered to be built in Scotland in the early 1890s for the Union Steamship Company of British Columbia Ltd. While the three steel vessels were fabricated by J. McArthur & Co., Glasgow, they weren't completed there. Instead the vessels were shipped in sections around Cape Horn to arrive in Vancouver where they were assembled.

Founded in November 1889, the Union Steamship Company was formed, "to supply the increasing demands for passengers and cargo to the outlying new settlements, sawmills, logging camps, stone quarries, agricultural and mining districts," according to Company historian Gerald Rushton. The company began operations with a small fleet operating in Burrard Inlet and consisting of the 57-foot paddle steamer SS *Leonora*, the 51-foot SS *Senator* and the 76-foot tug *Skidegate*, along with several scows. These vessels were primarily engaged in harbour towing and on the Moodyville-Hastings Mill ferry run. Then, in order to exploit the growing opportunities along the coast, capital was raised in the United Kingdom and three new steel ships were ordered.

The second of the trio completed was *Capilano*, which slid down the recently cleared shipway on Coal Harbour on December 5, 1891. She was 120 feet in length with a breadth of 22.2 feet, a depth of 9.6 feet and a gross tonnage listed as 231.1. Although *Capilano* was primarily intended for freight carriage (the builder guaranteed the vessel for 350 tons of deadweight cargo), she was also licensed, and had the deck space to berth 25 passengers.

Powered by a pair of compound steam engines built by Bow McLachlan & Co., Paisley, Scotland,

**Dyea Direct**

CHEAP RATES

**S. S. CAPILANO**

Will leave Victoria, B. C., direct for Dyea

**Saturday, Aug. 21**

Horses, $20 each.   Passengers, $10 each.
Freight, $10 per ton.
Passengers with three or more horses, FREE.

For further information, apply to
**S. V. CHRISTIAN, Agent,**
Roxwell Block.

The SS *Capilano* advertised cheap rates for passage from Victoria, BC, to Dyea, Alaska: "Passengers with three or more horses, FREE." This advertisement is probably from 1897. UNDERWATER ARCHAEOLOGICAL SOCIETY OF BRITISH COLUMBIA COLLECTION

*Capilano* was, according to Gerald Rushton in his book *Whistle Up the Inlet*, "powerfully engined, with large steel boilers for economic consumption." The estimated speed of the new steamer was 8 to 9 knots loaded, and 10 knots travelling light.

After running her trials in Burrard Inlet, on February 4, 1892, *Capilano* left for Victoria to fetch new boilers for the Moodyville Mill in Burrard Inlet. Her next job was carrying coal from Nanaimo. In 1894 both *Capilano* and *Coquitlam* were chartered to the New England Fish Company and participated in the development of the British Columbia halibut industry. During this time *Capilano* was also involved in transporting stone from quarries on Nelson Island and elsewhere to Victoria for the building of the new Parliament Buildings.

Three years later, when news of the rich gold strikes in the Klondike reached the outside world, hordes of miners arrived in British Columbia seeking transportation to Dyea and Skagway at the head of the Lynn Canal in Alaska. Gerald Rushton claimed that *Capilano* was the first Canadian steamer to leave a British Columbia port for the main gateway to the gold fields when she departed Vancouver July 22, 1897, with a full load of passengers, 69 head of cattle and 20 horses. *Capilano*, along with *Cutch* and *Coquitlam*, were to remain occupied with scheduled Skagway service from Victoria

When she departed from Vancouver in 1897, *Capilano* became the first Canadian steamer to leave a British Columbia port heading for the Klondike gold fields. In this photograph she is seen towing the paddlewheeler *Lightning* into the harbour at St. Michaels, Alaska, in 1899. VANCOUVER MARITIME MUSEUM NEG 1927

and Vancouver for two years. By 1900, as runs to southeast Alaska became more linked to the port of Seattle, there was a slackening in demand for service from a BC port.

As a result, *Capilano* was withdrawn and redirected to serve the expanding trade in British Columbia's northern waters where a mail contract had been approved for the Nass River. By the early 1900s, *Capilano* was making scheduled runs to northern connections while stopping at various fish canneries along the way. Once Union Steamship began constructing modern passenger vessels, both *Capilano* and *Coquitlam* were assigned entirely to cannery and freighting demands.

It was while operating in this service that *Capilano* left Vancouver early in the morning of September 29, 1915, carrying general cargo and with a crew of 16 aboard but without any passengers. She called in at two or three ports and by the evening of September 30 was proceeding to Van Anda on Texada Island to discharge some freight. The night was particularly dark with a considerable amount of smoke in the atmosphere, which was quite common at that time of the year as many logging companies were burning slash.

After rounding Scotch Fir Point (the northern point at the junction of Jervis Inlet with Malaspina Strait) Samuel Nelson, the ship's master, retired to his cabin for a short rest leaving the acting second mate, Fletcher Hemmonds, in charge. (Nelson was fatigued after spending a considerable amount of time on deck, making several landings and struggling to navigate through the smoky haze.)

Around 9:25 p.m., and about two miles from Van Anda, *Capilano* struck a submerged object. Most of the witnesses examined by the subsequent investigation into the ship's loss stated that they thought that the vessel had struck a log. The wreck commissioner and his assessors disagreed and pointed out that due to the dark and smoky conditions *Capilano* was probably further off coming round Scotch Fir Point than estimated, thus bringing her close in to the Texada shore where she may have struck a submerged rock, not a log. In making this observation, they noted that the master had been awakened by the sound of the whistle, and a short five-second echo bouncing off land. It brought him running into the wheelhouse to yell at the helmsman, "Haul her to the westward . . . Port!!"

Although it was suspected that *Capilano* had received serious damage, no leak was found and the coastal freighter continued on to Van Anda. She left there at about 11:00 p.m. and then, at about 1:30 a.m. on the morning of October 1, while steering east by north, she began listing heavily to port into a southeasterly blowing hard with rain and haze. Water two feet deep was now discovered in the lower hold.

Captain Nelson was hopeful that his ship could still make Campbell River but the hull was badly punctured and, as the water rose, the ship's condition became more perilous. Also, a number of drums of gasoline in the hold began washing back and forth with the movement of the ship, and fears that the drums would eventually open her seams convinced the crew to take to a large lifeboat at 3:00 a.m.

*Capilano* sank at 5:30 a.m. on October 1, 1915, five miles WSW of Harwood Island according to her Wreck Register entry. The crew rowed easterly in search of land and eventually reached Indian Point on the west end of Savary Island—but not before they had watched their ship slip beneath the waves. They gave vivid descriptions of the steamship's demise; of how her lights remained ablaze as she sank and how, just before she went to the bottom, the steam whistle gave a final, solitary blast.

A newspaper account of the day stated that *Capilano*, valued at $30,000, "had a cargo worth an additional $8,000 or $10,000, consisting chiefly of cannery supplies, gasoline and lumber." The Union Steamship Company had the vessel itself insured for 5,000 pounds sterling at the time of the loss.

In its attempt to unravel what caused the sinking, the court investigating the circumstances leading up to the loss was of the opinion that the submerged object *Capilano* struck the night before was a rock, some of which may have been carried away with her. The rock, along with coal in the hold, probably plugged the hole punched in the vessel initially, allowing little water to penetrate. However, once the ship left Van Anda and encountered increasing wind and rough water, it was suggested, whatever was blocking the hole worked itself loose and allowed the vessel to fill with water.

Since there was only speculation, and no evidence, as to what the submerged object indeed was, Samuel Nelson was given the benefit of the doubt and his master's certificate was returned to him. The court did censure Nelson though, "for retiring to his cabin under the conditions of the weather then prevailing, and leaving an uncertified man . . . in charge of the ship." The acting second mate, Fletcher Hemmonds, was criticized for not calling the master under the existing circumstances and nearing the next port of call, Van Anda.

Since he didn't possess a certificate, the court warned him that once he obtained a certificate he certainly would be held responsible for similar, future incidents.

The final resting place of the old Union Steamship Company freighter is on the bottom in some 120 feet of water on the south side of Grant Reefs located between Savary and Harwood Islands in the Strait of Georgia. Apparently, once the investigation into the loss was completed, no known commercial salvage was ever attempted on *Capilano*, probably because she was in deep water and was transporting goods considered of no great value. She would remain undisturbed on the bottom by Grant Reefs for some 57 years.

In 1972, a Lund fisherman, Neil Gustafson, pulled up a piece of metal railing from an unknown wreck on Grant Reefs. He subsequently reported the find to diver Rick McIntosh, and McIntosh and his diving buddy, Courtenay Powell, became the first to dive the wreck. Later, McIntosh returned to the wreck site with fellow diver Bob Briggs of Powell River in an attempt to identify the mystery ship. In the course of some 15 dives they retrieved a number of items, including 16 portholes, the ship's compass, bottles, china and a marble sink, but what they were most excited about was finding the ship's strong box. Once ashore they broke it open, only to discover that their hoped-for treasure consisted of bills of lading and four pennies dated 1907, 1911, 1912 and 1914.

While McIntosh and Powell were successful in keeping the location a secret for a while, by the mid-1970s a number of others had learned where the wreck was and began diving it. Now that it was well known, especially after being written up in *Diver Magazine* in December 1981, the secret was out: *Capilano* was considered the best wreck dive on the BC coast.

Finally, with the increasing traffic to the site, the Underwater Archaeological Society of BC was contacted and on June 9, 1984, an information/education plaque was placed on the stern to encourage divers to respect the heritage site. On November 6, 1985, the *Capilano* officially became a Designated Provincial Heritage Site through a Provincial Order-in-Council.

Nonetheless, despite the fact that the *Capilano* is a designated historic site—and it is illegal to remove anything—it was reported some years ago that a group of divers had made off with the ship's wheel, a destructive act that is entirely unacceptable by today's diving standards. Hopefully, as more dive groups continue to visit the fascinating and beautiful wreck site of *Capilano* (the entire hull is festooned with white plumose anemones) they will have the decency to "remove nothing, leave only bubbles."

Colin Stares, a diver with the Underwater Archaeological Society of BC, explores the wreck *Capilano*, resting at a point midway between Savary Island and Cape Mudge. JACQUES MARC PHOTO, 2007

# Chapter 8

# Wooden Ships: Wartime Shipbuilding that Fuelled Victoria's Economy, 1917–1918

Streetcar passengers returning from an evening in Gorge Park witnessed "a vast fairyland of lights" from the Point Ellice Bridge during the summer of 1918. The source of this spectacle was the night shift of wartime shipbuilding underway in Victoria Harbour. Beneath powerful searchlights the huge gantry derricks of the Foundation Company lifted their loads over a number of wooden ships in various stages of production.

The American company, a specialist in constructing bridge piers, industrial foundations and mine shafts, was in the midst of finishing a contract for five wooden cargo steamships for Canada's Imperial Munitions Board (IMB). The names of the new vessels on the stocks—*War Songhee*, *War Babine*, *War Camchin*, *War Masset* and *War Nanoose*—left no doubt as to their intended purpose.

The year before, the *Daily Colonist* had forewarned that the old Songhees reserve was about to undergo a transformation "in the relentless march of industrial progress." As the city entered a new era of shipbuilding, old landmarks were to make room for newer monuments, with the *Colonist* reporter prophesying that "never again will the curling smoke wreaths from the Indian campfires be seen floating through the treetops."

The Imperial Munitions Board saw the West Coast as an untapped source of shipbuilding potential after war losses incurred in the North Atlantic had begun to reach crisis proportions. Between May 1916 and January 1917, more than 1,150 ships were sunk. When Germany declared unrestricted U-boat warfare in February 1917, the rate of these losses more than doubled and another 2,566 ships went to the bottom by year's end.

Shipping experts from England, Canada and the United States arrived in British Columbia looking for a solution to an impending disaster. While some steel shipbuilding was already underway on the West Coast, steel plate was imported at great cost. As a result, the international group proceeded to inspect some five-masted wooden auxiliary schooners already under construction in Victoria's Upper Harbour.

The Cameron brothers, owners of a large Victoria sawmill, had leased the foreshore next to the Point Ellice Bridge in July 1916 and had built a shipyard. The deepwater sailers now under construction were a desperate attempt to deliver their wood products to overseas markets. The group was visibly impressed with

The building of wooden ships, such as these on the ways at the Foundation Company Shipyard in Victoria Harbour, created a demand for enormous quantities of timbers and planking, keeping local sawmills humming and thousands of loggers employed in British Columbia forests. COURTESY OF ROYAL BC MUSEUM, BC ARCHIVES C-05376

the efforts of Cameron-Genoa Mills Shipbuilders Ltd., declaring the motor-sailers on the ways ". . . the very best . . . turned out anywhere in the world."

After hearing these glowing testimonials, the IMB wasted no time in awarding contracts for the construction of both steel and wooden cargo steamers. The 27 wooden ships were to be three-island single deck vessels of 2,800 deadweight tons with dimensions of 250 x 43.5 x 23 feet. Before it had completed the sixth and last of its own auxiliary schooners, *Beatrice Castle*, Cameron-Genoa Mills Shipbuilders Ltd. had an order on hand for four of the new vessels. *War Haida*, *War Skeena*, *War Stikine* and *War Yukon*, all standard Canadian wooden cargo steamers, were to be built out of Douglas fir and powered by triple expansion engines.

With this development it appeared that Cameron-Genoa Mills was firmly established in the shipbuilding business, but in reality their success was to be short lived. Jaime Cameron, a son of one of the founding fathers, attributed this to a change in the provincial government, which subsequently cut off their financing. Another factor that may have played a part in the Cameron brothers' change of fortune was a serious fire that gutted their sawmill in June 1917.

After receiving a 60-ship contract from the French government in 1918 the Foundation Company's British Columbia operation took over the Camerons' shipyard. Their vast operations now included all the

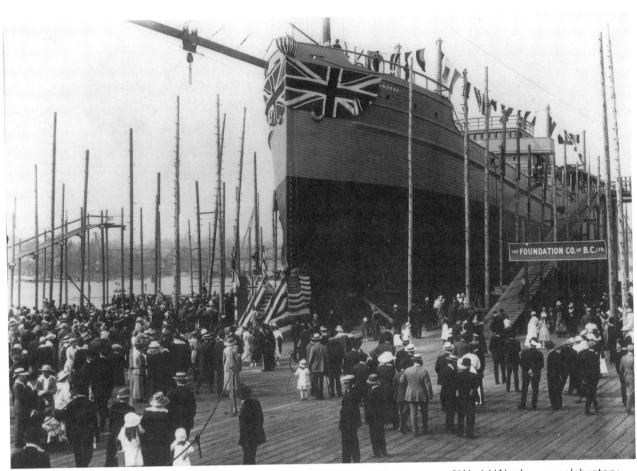

The launchings of large wood cargo ships in Victoria Harbour in the later years of World War I were celebratory affairs attended by large audiences. The *Victoria Daily Colonist* of August 30, 1918, noted that the entry of the *War Nanoose* into the water on September 9 was to be a particularly noteworthy event since ". . . the Foundation Company has decided to combine the launching of the last vessel of the old Imperial Munitions Board programme with the laying of the two keels of the first two of the twenty ships under contract for the French Government." COURTESY OF ROYAL BC MUSEUM, BC ARCHIVES F-04535

harbour foreshore from Point Ellice Bridge to what is the site of today's Songhees development. While the company also built yards in Tacoma and Portland for the construction of 20 auxiliary schooners each, the Victoria operation received the wooden steamship portion of the order. These 20 ships, with approximate dimensions of 260 x 46 x 22 feet and a deadweight tonnage of 3,000, were somewhat larger than their IMB counterparts and were fitted with twin screws driven by triple expansion engines.

Although the vessels' stated loaded speed was 10 knots, they usually averaged between 12 and 13 knots in their trial runs. One worker recalled that the resilience and strength of the wooden hulls were put to the test at the Ogden Point outfitting plant when a cable holding aloft a 5-ton boiler being prepared for installation broke. When the hull was checked for damage, there wasn't any.

Since the Point Ellice yard was allowed to retain its supervisory staff and yard crew, a rivalry developed with the Point Hope yard, stimulating production in the process. If keels happened to be laid at the same time, the race was on to see which yard would be the first to launch. The local community was kept apprised of this friendly competition and other company news via a weekly newspaper—*Shipyard Shavings*—published every Saturday and available at some newsstands. When a magnificent clubhouse was erected (close to where the Princess Mary restaurant stood for years) the paper professed that it was "symbolic of the wonderful spirit which animates [*sic*] from the Foundation activities."

This industrial *esprit de corps* was further cultivated by sporting activities and entertainment programs. The company formed baseball and football teams and, it was rumoured, even went as far as hiring local sport stars as ringers to boost morale in Tacoma and Portland. Archie Wills, a *Colonist* reporter, later recalled that the Foundation Company sponsored a lacrosse team that returned from Winnipeg with the Mann Cup. The company also had a band that entertained employees during lunch hour and performed in the community after hours. When one of the sleek grey hulls was finally ready for launching, the band, under the baton of Lou Turner, played a rousing rendition of the *Marseillaise*.

The employees gladly participated in the festive atmosphere and by early 1919 the fortnightly payroll was $230,000. By the time the last of the ships, *Nouvelle Ecosse*, had been launched, on October 9, 1919, the entire French contract had paid out over $5.5 million in wages. Archie Wills (along with war weary soldiers returning from the Western Front in France) was surprised to find the city prospering and shipyard employees "rolling in money, even to the use of . . . motorcars!"

The unprecedented prosperity was all too brief and with the last of the ships on its way to Le Havre, France, the once bustling Inner Harbour began to look like an industrial wasteland, but the most notable change was the loss of a large payroll to Victoria's economy. Chris Cholberg, a recent Norwegian immigrant to British Columbia, attempted to revive shipbuilding in 1919 as a government-supported project to relieve unemployment, which was rampant among demobilized servicemen, but after the fourth sailing

Workers at the Foundation Company Shipyard in Victoria, BC, look contented as they pose in front of a wooden ship under construction. The city and its shipyards were experiencing a period of great prosperity. COURTESY OF ROYAL BC MUSEUM, BC ARCHIVES F-02253

ship, *S.F. Tolmie*, was completed in 1920, it was realized that commercial sailing was no longer financially viable. The launching of the four-masted barquentine only served to signal the end of large wooden shipbuilding in Victoria.

Even the Imperial Munitions Board's wood cargo steamer program proved to be a disappointment: the 27 ships were built of unseasoned softwood and most were either scrapped or lost to fire or marine perils by 1925. (The lone exception was the *War Yukon*, which managed to survive as a barge up until 1937.)

While the ships were somewhat of a commercial failure, the high wages earned during their construction attracted thousands to shipyards throughout the Lower Mainland and Victoria. Supplying the enormous quantities of timbers and planking needed for the ships—around 50 million board feet annually—also kept local sawmills humming and thousands of loggers employed in British Columbia forests. Wood ships kept Victoria's economy alive through the Great War and the province's vast first-growth forests were somewhat reduced in the process.

# Chapter 9

# From Lumber Freighter
# to Floating Cannery to Beach Hulk:
# The *Laurel Whalen*, 1917

Other than a hawse pipe sticking out of the mud at the end of the breakwater, there's nothing left to be seen of *Laurel Whalen* at the old Comox Logging & Railway Company booming grounds at Royston. The five-masted auxiliary schooner was originally one of six built at the Cameron-Genoa Mills Shipbuilders Ltd. Victoria shipyard during the Great War. The other five that slipped down the Point Ellice ways in 1917 were *Margaret Haney*, *Esquimalt*, *Jean Steedman*, *Beatrice Castle* and the infamous *Malahat*, which went on to gain notoriety as a mother ship to the rum-running fleet off California and Mexico.

These unusual wood sailers, with their two Swedish Bolinder semi-diesel engines and twin screws, were built in response to a wartime tonnage shortage. When the heavy losses to U-boats during the First World War drained steamships away from the Pacific and disrupted commercial shipping in the process, British Columbia's lumber industry was already suffering from overproduction and poor demand. (A little known fact is that while there may have been more tonnage lost to U-boats in World War II, more actual vessels were lost during the First World War.) By 1915, with virtually no shipping available for the offshore cargo trade, British Columbia sawmill owners found themselves in a desperate situation. In 1895 BC mills accounted for 35 percent of west coast North America lumber exports to Australia; through 1912 to 1914 this average was down to less than 5 percent, and as the war progressed the situation only worsened.

While British Columbia sawmills struggled to stay alive, US sawmills throughout Washington and Oregon were busy filling orders for foreign buyers. What kept American mills busy trying to meet the demand was the fact their owners had had the foresight to build up their own fleet of lumber carriers to transport their product across the Pacific. As a consequence, lumbermen such as the Cameron brothers, who owned a large sawmill in Victoria's Inner Harbour, quickly came to the conclusion that they needed to build their own fleet of freighters in order to save their languishing enterprises. (James Oscar and Donald Officer Cameron, who were originally from Tennessee as it happened, had no prior experience in shipbuilding, let alone lumbering, when they immigrated to British Columbia.)

In early 1916 the Camerons, along with shipping interests, the Manufacturer's Association and other worried sawmill owners, began lobbying the provincial government for financial assistance to build a Canadian-owned commercial sailing fleet. With the passage of the Shipbuilding Assistance

Upon the launch of the *Laurel Whalen* into Victoria harbour, Victoria's *Daily Colonist* reported the following on March 25, 1917: "Amidst the hoarse blasts of whistles and the cheering of thousands of spectators, the gaily be-decked hull of the auxiliary schooner *Laurel Whalen* glided speedily down the ways." RONALD GREENE COLLECTION

Act in May of that year, the Cameron Lumber Company, in conjunction with the Genoa Bay Lumber Company (also owned by the Camerons), utilized government promises of loans and bonus provisions to create its own shipbuilding arm, Cameron-Genoa Mills Shipbuilders Ltd. Unfortunately the two brothers encountered financial difficulties and their shipbuilding venture on the southwest side of the Point Ellice Bridge was short lived. The shipyard was turned over to the Foundation Company in September 1918, but not before the Camerons' operation had completed its own six schooners as well as four wooden cargo steamers.

Ship plans reveal that these *Mabel Brown* class schooners didn't stint on wood and used massive timbers and planks in their construction. To start with, the new ships measured some 240 to 245 feet in length and 1,350 to 1,550 gross tons (the *Laurel Whalen* was 240.5 feet and displaced 1,357 tons.) The keel and nine keelsons used for structural strength were made of 20-inch square timbers. Frames of 12 inches square were doubled and spaced at 32 inches. Hanging knees were cut from naturally grown crooks of Douglas fir. The outside planking varied in size from 4 inches square on the bulwarks to 7 x 11 inches near the waterline, with ceiling planking as large as 14 x 16 inches. Planks were fastened with hardwood treenails, while driftbolts of 1–1.5 inches in diameter studded the hull.

These were "bald-headed" schooners since they were lacking in topsails. *Laurel Whalen* was rigged with fore, main, mizzen, jigger and spanker sails, a fore staysail, and inner, outer and flying jibs. Art Jones, writing in 1954, recalled that the *Mabel Brown* class vessels were ". . . good sea-boats, and had good lines . . . . After being in the Australian square-rigger grain ships, these five-masted schooners seemed like a sailor's

With masts and rigging raised, the *Laurel Whalen* is pictured here in 1917, across Victoria harbour from the Cameron-Genoa Mills Shipbuilders Ltd. yard located off the southwest corner of the Point Ellice Bridge. COURTESY OF ROYAL BC MUSEUM, BC ARCHIVES G-3571

dream of heaven. A wheelhouse, electric light, steam to hoist the anchor, compressed air winches to hoist sail. No brass and no varnish work to look after. No chipping hammer. One yard (swung from the foremast) instead of ten or fifteen, and only two persons on the ship who knew what it was for. One was the skipper, the other myself. There were no gaff topsails so the boys didn't need to go any higher aloft after dark than the top bunks."

Hugh "Red" Garling, who sailed on *Laurel Whalen's* sister ship, *Malahat*, was struck by the great expanse of deck—some 200 feet from fo'c'sle to poop—and the enormous flexing in her hull; the hogging and sagging as well as twisting, especially in a quartering sea. "In the fo'c'sle, or below, all about you was the dissonance of sounds her timbers made as they worked and resisted the flexing."

Unfortunately the Armistice of November 1918 was followed by a post-war economic depression, and an oversupply of steamships that were no longer required for the war effort flooded the commercial market. The subsequent drop in freight rates soon brought an end to viable commercial sail. As a consequence, the six Cameron-Genoa Mills auxiliary schooners built for the Canada West Coast Navigation Company ended up seeing little active service in the deep-sea lumber trade.

On her first lumber voyage, in June 1917, *Laurel Whalen* sailed for Port Adelaide, Australia, with a cargo of over 1.5 million board feet aboard. On her second, and last, lumber voyage out to Australia in the spring of 1918, she experienced a plague of labour problems amongst the crew while mechanical breakdowns bedevilled the schooner. Finally, on her return voyage back to the West Coast, *Laurel Whalen* ran into heavy seas and her rigging was torn away. Since her Bolinder auxiliaries had already broken down in

Australia, she was effectively disabled by the time she was able to limp into Tahiti. A survey there revealed that teredo worms (burrowing, wood-digesting molluscs) were well established in her hull.

After sitting derelict in the tropics for a few months, the troubled vessel was retrieved early in 1919 by the powerful steam tug *Hercules*, dispatched from San Francisco. When the tug arrived in Vancouver Harbour with the *Whalen* on the towline, the *Vancouver Daily World* proclaimed, "The tug established a record for towing on the Pacific and brought the vessel to her native coast without a mishap of any kind." However, according to the *Vancouver Province*, within days of tying up, the schooner was embroiled in a "great mass of insurance claims," the ship was "in a pretty spongy state below the waterline," and ". . . has had five different crews and been delayed for months by weather and repairs . . . "

In a perilous state, *Laurel Whalen* seemed fated to join the scores of retired sailing vessels sitting on their anchor chains in quiet backwaters all along the west coast of North America. Instead, in December 1920, R.P. Butchart bought the ship and converted her into a cement barge. Butchart owned the BC Cement Company, the operators of a large plant on the Malahat side of Saanich Inlet, Vancouver Island. (His Tod Inlet quarry is the site of today's Butchart Gardens.)

However, the local industrialist only held onto the retired schooner for a short time, and in November 1923, *Harbour & Shipping* magazine noted that ". . . the *Laurel Whalen* underwent repairs at Victoria Machinery Depot, and has been purchased by the Somerville Cannery interests in Vancouver, to be used as a cannery tender." At this time, she was probably shorn of what was left of her masts, rigging and engines, if the Butchart interests hadn't already done so. The new owner, canneryman Francis Millerd of Vancouver, apparently had no intention of using the schooner as a tender; instead, he took advantage of an obscure Fisheries Department regulation to convert *Laurel Whalen* into a floating fish cannery. Since Millerd was able to tow his fish processing facility around the coast to one fish run after another, owners of land-based canneries feared that he would eventually put them out of business. Pressure on the Fisheries Department finally produced an ultimatum ordering Millerd to pick one location—and stay anchored there.

A young Frederick Corneille got a job as a tally man on *Laurel Whalen* one summer in the early 1920s when the hulk was anchored in Ferguson Bay in the Queen Charlotte Islands (Haida Gwaii). Completely self-contained, the cannery had a steam plant with two canning lines and began the season with 10,000 cases of empty cans aboard. Every 10 days the Canadian National steamer *Prince John* came alongside to load the full cans and drop off a supply of empties. Corneille recalled that the crew packed some 40,000 cases in 25 days of operation that August. He claimed that the $600 he earned that summer was the most money he was to make until sometime after the Second World War. (Frederick Corneille, or "Cornie" as he was called, became a deckhand on Union Steamships in 1926 and eventually went on to become a Chief Officer. He also served in a corvette during the war and retired from the navy as a Lieutenant RCN(R).)

When *Laurel Whalen*'s licence finally expired in 1929, Corneille thought the schooner-cannery was laid up in fresh water, either at Lake Washington or up the Fraser River. (Fresh water deters most marine wood borers, such as teredo worms, which thrive in salt water.) As it happened, former Langley resident Glen Olson was a boy when *Laurel Whalen* and the Victoria-built four-master *S.F. Tolmie* were laid up for the winter at Ewans Cannery, near Lion Island in the Fraser River. Glen's father, Sig Olson, was a watchman for BC Packers, which apparently chartered the old hulls as pilchard scows. Around 1936, Sig was at the wheel when the *Whalen* was towed out of the river to Vancouver.

The ship's 1924 registry document reveals that *Laurel Whalen* remained in Millerd's hands until he sold the floating cannery to Alfred Robie Bissett in March 1936. This may explain why marine writer Norman Hacking said he remembered seeing the hulk in Coal Harbour in the late 1930s. Bissett was manager of

Canneryman Francis Millerd, after purchasing the *Laurel Whalen* hulk in November 1923, took advantage of an obscure Fisheries Department clause to convert the retired lumber schooner into a floating salmon cannery. Here, the converted *Laurel Whalen* is operating in this capacity at Ferguson Bay, Queen Charlotte Islands. FRANCIS MILLERD COLLECTION

BC Wharf and Machinery Co. Ltd. located at 1901 West Georgia, a block east of Stanley Park. The Bissetts also owned the Britannia Sand & Gravel Co. Ltd., located at the same address. If they didn't have plans for converting the hulk into a barge, they may have been involved in conversion work for a new floating venture.

On May 11, 1936, an article in a Vancouver newspaper reported that the *Laurel Whalen* was being fitted out as a cabaret. "Permission to anchor the craft in English Bay has been granted by the port authority, and the old *Laurel Whalen* will soon resound to the saws and hammers of the carpenters who fit her up with dance floor and other accommodations. The boat will be anchored a few feet outside the half mile line, just beyond the boundary which the city police have authority."

Later, the *Comox Argus* named the man behind the scheme as none other than Tommy Burns, a Canadian who was the heavyweight boxing champion of the world between 1906 and 1908. Burns invested his prize money in business ventures, including British pubs, a New York speakeasy and, apparently, the floating cabaret. Unfortunately for the local party crowd, the authorities were opposed to the venture. As the *Argus* reported: "But somehow or other, no licence could be procured; and so after two nights of revelry she was deserted."

With their ambitious plan now dead in the water, the owners put the hulk up for sale but were also considering wrecking her on a beach for scrap metal and the firewood in her hull. Instead, on August 12, 1936, *Laurel Whalen* was sold to the Comox Logging & Railway Company for $452.63. After her varied career, she was destined to become the first in a collection of retired ships used as a breakwater at the company's Royston log dump and booming grounds.

On August 20, 1936, the *Comox Argus* reported on the tow across the Strait of Georgia from Vancouver

By the 1990s there was not much left to identify the *Laurel Whalen* at Royston other than a tangled litter of drift bolts and two hawse pipes (where the anchor chains pass through the hull) sticking out of the mud next to the rusted hull of the CPR steam tug *Nanoose*. RICK JAMES PHOTO, 1992

The lumber schooner's steering quadrant identifies what would have been the stern section of the *Laurel Whalen*. Sometime around 2000, Primex Forest Products, who were still using the site to store logs destined for their sawmill on the Courtenay River, extended the rock ballast breakwater out over the remains of the *Laurel Whalen*. RICK JAMES PHOTO, 1992

to Comox Harbour by the big outside tug *Gleeful*, owned by Comox Logging's sister company, the Canadian Tugboat Company. "She was turned over to the tug *Gleeful* to tow to Royston. A west wind sprang up and the old hulk, swinging sluggishly in the sea, pulled hard against her fate and the *Gleeful* had a tussle with her in the storm during which her only remaining mast snapped off and went through the cabin." Tug and tow finally made into the protected waters behind Goose Spit where the hulk was tied up to the company's log booms. There, the small (40 feet registered length) harbour tug *Joyful* put the towline on to take her across Comox harbour to Royston.

Once *Laurel Whalen* was secured to pilings, Royston's boom camp foreman set to work scuttling her. "Mr. Hugh Cliffe and his gang bored four-inch holes in her hull last night, and she gradually settled down on the beach where she will be a feature of the landscape for years to come."

Charles Nordin, whose father was skipper of the *Joyful*, went along for the excitement of watching the sinking of the old auxiliary schooner that day. He recalls that it took a major amount of doing and "there was a lot of ki-yiing and bad language coming from Hughie Cliffe during the process to get her to lay exactly upon her resting place."

Nordin also has fond memories of rowing out to the hulk with a buddy while it was still anchored off Comox Spit and remembers, in particular, the vessel's beautiful hardwood dance floors. The two lads crawled around inside the ship while fantasizing that they were taking part in an episode from *Tom Sawyer*.

The lumber schooner's bones have lain off the small community of Royston on Vancouver Island for over 60 years now and the weather and sea have long since taken their due. While she was still afloat, and even after she was scuttled at Royston, she was able to find useful service in a variety of roles along the West Coast. Still, the purpose for which she was originally intended—a life under sail, deepwater lumber trading—was short lived.

Nonetheless, while the *Mabel Brown* class motor sailers, such as *Laurel Whalen*, were never commercially successful in the offshore lumber trade, they did prove effective in rescuing British Columbia's languishing coastal sawmills from impending disaster. The 50 million board feet of lumber required annually during the First World War for a crash shipbuilding program of auxiliary schooners and wooden steamships helped pull a young British Columbia lumber industry through to better times. In 1946 the Cameron brothers were able to sell their successful sawmilling operation in Victoria to Toronto promoter E.P. Taylor, who was busy buying up West Coast mills and timber. Taylor eventually combined all his acquisitions into the timber giant BC Forest Products Ltd.

*Chapter 10*

# West Coast Gale Claims
# HMCS *Galiano*, 1918

Abrief signal—"Holds full of water; send help"—was picked up by the wireless operator at Triangle Island off the northwest end of Vancouver Island near Cape Scott on October 30, 1918. The distress call was from the Royal Canadian Navy's (RCN) 393-ton, 162-foot patrol steamer HMCS *Galiano*. The vessel was caught in open water as the first serious fall storm hit the West Coast.

The RCN had come into existence only seven years earlier with the passing of the Naval Service Act on May 4, 1910. Other than two submarines secretly purchased from the Americans by British Columbia's provincial government in 1914, there were just two outdated cruisers, *Niobe* and the *Rainbow*, that served as the only offensive warships during the Great War. The bulk of the Naval Service was made up of a motley assortment of vessels acquired when the RCN incorporated the fishery patrol, hydrographic, tidal survey and wireless telegraphic services of the Department of Marine and Fisheries with the passage of the

The brief signal "Holds full of water; send help" was picked up by the wireless operator at Triangle Island off the northwest end of Vancouver Island near Cape Scott on October 30, 1918. The distress call was from the Royal Canadian Navy's 393-ton, 162-foot patrol steamer HMCS *Galiano*. CFB ESQUIMALT NAVAL & MILITARY MUSEUM

Act. Although they maintained their regular peacetime duties, the primary role of these ships during the First World War was to serve as patrol craft, minesweepers and examination vessels.

*Galiano* and her sister ship *Malaspina* were originally built in Dublin Dockyard, Ireland, in 1913 as fishery patrol craft for Canada's Dominion Government. The ships were named for Don Alejandro Malaspina and Don Dionisio Alcala Galiano, both officers in the Spanish navy who commanded exploratory expeditions to the northwest coast of the Americas in the 1790s. *Galiano* maintained her role as a fishery patrol ship until the First World War began and was then assigned to Esquimalt as a naval patrol vessel, but it was while performing a task as a lighthouse tender late in 1918 that the ship came to a tragic end.

An order was received in October to proceed to Triangle Island with supplies as the wireless station there was nearly out of the fuel needed to run its power plant. *Malaspina* was scheduled to leave with stores and supplies for the wireless stations and lighthouses on the West Coast but the morning the ship was to begin the voyage her bow was crumpled in an accident at the jetty. The supplies were quickly transferred to *Galiano* even though the ship had just returned from the Queen Charlotte Islands to Esquimalt and needed boiler work and repairs to her tail shaft.

Able Seaman James Aird (like a number of his fellow shipmates on what was to be their ship's last voyage) had misgivings about the voyage. A letter Aird posted at Alert Bay hinted at nagging fears of impending disaster. Addressed to Mrs. Ranns, "mother" of the Sailor's Club at Esquimalt where the Able Seaman from Calgary bunked while ashore, the missive noted that the *Galiano* had run into foul weather after leaving Vancouver. Aird went on to state that they had already heard that the Canadian Pacific Railway boat *Princess Sophia* was experiencing difficulties as a result of a bad storm.

(As it happened, these "difficulties" were to result in one of the worst marine disasters ever in the Pacific Northwest. On October 24 the CPR's coastal steamer ran aground on Vanderbilt Reef in Lynn Canal and during a gale the next day slid off into the depths taking all 343 souls aboard with her.)

Aird added that he was dreading the trip across to Triangle Island, as it meant crossing one of the most dangerous stretches of water along the West Coast—Queen Charlotte Sound—in foul weather. Adding to his worries was the fact that many of the ship's complement were absent, as the worst epidemic of the twentieth century, the Spanish flu, had just arrived on the West Coast. A.B. Aird added "I am not worried for myself, but I hate a green crew . . ."

Knowing that any of *Galiano*'s regular crew that could get down to the ship were going to be desperately needed, Aird had walked aboard still wearing several plasters applied by Mrs. Ranns. Others who were well enough to sail included the ship's commander Lieutenant Robert Mayes Pope, Royal Naval Canadian Volunteer Reserve (RNCVR), the bo'sun, Chief Petty Officer James Vinnecombe, chief artificer engineer Frank Greenshields and the wireless telegraph operator, Michael Neary. (In an unusual twist of fate, Neary's brother Jack happened to be one of the wireless operators stationed at Triangle Island when *Galiano*'s distress call was received. Contrary to what many later writers claimed, it was Arthur Ashdown Green who actually copied the doomed ship's message, not Jack Neary, who was asleep at the time.)

Lieutenant Pope had commanded *Galiano* since its arrival on the West Coast in 1913. An able and experienced mariner, Pope had established an impressive career before joining the RCN. He had served on sailing ships, East India Company steamers and a Royal Navy cruiser, and had also made several voyages as third officer on the Canadian Pacific Railway's oceanic liner *Empress of India*.

So many of the ship's complement were sick that the navy was forced to borrow crew from *Malaspina* and assign men from the Esquimalt Navy Yard to serve. Joseph Gilbert arrived off HMCS *Rainbow* and

This portrait shows the crew of the ill-fated HMCS *Galiano*. The lucky ones missed the voyage. Many of the ship's complement were overcome with the Spanish flu, the worst epidemic of the 20th century, and stayed ashore recuperating. CFB ESQUIMALT NAVAL & MILITARY MUSEUM VR 999.684.1

replaced the ship's regular chief officer, Ernest Alcock, who had been taken ill. Leading Seaman Alex Munroe, who had served on *Galiano* earlier but had since been working in the dockyard and on *Malaspina*, replaced *Galiano*'s sick quartermaster. Able Seaman William King, who was in the dockyard armoury at the time, signed on along with 16-year-old Roderick McLeod who joined the ship as captain's boy. Young McLeod wrote home that he feared he was about to leave on a dangerous trip.

When *Galiano* arrived at Triangle Island, the ship was to pick up the housekeeper, Miss Emily Brunton, and Sydney Eliott, one of the operators. It was while she was performing these duties that a gale began to rise. At the last moment, Eliott discovered his leave was cancelled and he returned to the station. The last of the supplies were unloaded in a hurry and Miss Brunton was taken on board *Galiano*'s work boat, which returned to the ship. *Galiano* then pointed its bow northward to its next stop, Ikeda Head on the Queen Charlotte Islands.

The *Daily Colonist* of Thursday, October 31, reported that the patrol boat left Triangle Island at 5:00 p.m. on Tuesday with a fierce southwest gale building. The paper noted that naval officials estimated that when her distress signal was received, at 3:00 a.m. on Wednesday morning, the ship should have been within visual range of the light on Cape St. James on the far southern end of the Queen Charlotte Islands, 95 miles from Triangle Island.

In an attempt to explain why no further signals were received, it was suggested that her aerials may have been carried away or the set of dynamos in the engine room powering the wireless equipment might have been put out of commission. The *Colonist* also spoke with local mariners who agreed that the stretch of water *Galiano* was in was the worst anywhere along the Pacific coast.

Among the vessels that responded to the SOS and raced to the scene were the American tug *Tatoosh*, the Grand Trunk Pacific tug *Lorne*, trawler *G.E. Foster* and three whalers from the Rose Harbour whaling station. Anxious relatives spent a long four days waiting to hear news of the lost vessel. Then on Sunday, November 3, the *Daily Colonist* ran a full-page article featuring short biographies of those aboard *Galiano* along with some photographs of crew and officers. The article opened by saying the only traces of *Galiano* found were a lifebelt, a skylight with a ditty bag containing a few articles of clothing owned by stoker George Musty hanging from it, and three bodies. The body of Leading Seaman Wilfred Ebbs was recovered by *G.E. Foster* 28 miles south of Cape St. James and the bodies of Stoker Arthur Hume and Able Seaman James Aird were found about 15 miles east of Danger Rocks by the whaler *Brown*.

When *G.E. Foster* arrived in Prince Rupert, her captain gave his account of what he thought had happened. He felt the vessel had probably foundered in heavy seas and he stressed the fact that, "the whole of the Hecate Straits is just one mass of foam . . . with a tremendous sea running." He went on to suggest that *Galiano* probably shipped a large wave and the weight of the water rolling around inside had caused her bulkheads to give way, causing the ship to roll and ship more seas. It appeared that *Galiano* had gone down fast; the lifebelts and clothing of the men they picked up looked as if they had been put on in a hurry as the belts were not fastened properly.

Today, Canadians can view a memorial to this maritime disaster in the far southeast corner of Ross Bay cemetery along Victoria's waterfront. The large block of granite overlooking Juan de Fuca Strait has chiselled into it the names of 36 crew and officers serving in HMCS *Galiano* whose bodies were never found. The memorial also happens to commemorate the only warship lost by the Royal Canadian Navy in the First World War. Sadly, HMCS *Galiano* disappeared only a few days before the signing of the Armistice on November 11, 1918, which signalled the end of the Great War and four years of slaughter in the trenches of France.

**Footnote:**

In September 2007, Jim Hume, columnist with the Victoria *Times Colonist,* attempted to verify whether there was indeed a Miss Emma Mary "Emily" Brunton who boarded HMCS *Galiano* at Triangle Light.

After some assistance from his readership, it was discovered that, according to the 1917 Victoria directory, in 1916 an Emma Brunton, dressmaker, was living at 1124 Fort St., Victoria, where she was possibly a housekeeper for one Charles Long, manager of the New Brunswick Cigar Shop. That same year,

A memorial to all those whose bodies were never found following the loss of HMCS *Galiano* was erected in the far southeast corner of Victoria's historic Ross Bay cemetery overlooking the Juan de Fuca Strait. RICK JAMES PHOTO

at the age of 35, she was hired as a housekeeper by bachelor radio operators at Triangle Island, who were probably tired of their own cooking and cleaning.

Thanks to Frank Statham, who maintains a wealth of information on early coastal radio stations, Miss Brunton was reported to be "rather plumpish" in appearance and that, "to the chagrin" of the bachelor operators on the island who pooled their money to hire her, ". . . she soon had them organized. They had to dress for dinner with clean shirts, ties and jackets, and their shoes had to be polished. As compensation she was an excellent cook and their dwelling was kept spotless."

On October 29, 1918, after being relieved of her duties as a housekeeper, Brunton was seen boarding HMCS *Galiano*. She was never seen alive again. Records of the Supreme Court of BC reveal that after the court authorized that Emma Mary Brunton be presumed dead, her $716.69 in bank savings was ordered to be shared equally between her mother, two sisters and a brother in Glossop, England.

# Chapter 11

# Chinese Junks Make Landfall on the BC Coast: 1922 and 1939

There's always been talk drifting about the docks about how it would have been entirely possible, sometime in the past, for an Oriental vessel to sail or drift across the North Pacific to make landfall somewhere along our West Coast. When two actually completed this remarkable feat—one sailing into Victoria's busy harbour in 1922 and the other ending its arduous voyage in the remote Central Coast mill town of Ocean Falls in 1939—they caused quite a sensation.

**The Amoy**

In the article "Crowds Throng to see Chinese Junk," the *Victoria Daily Colonist* of September 21, 1922, reported that ". . . skipper and ship were well nigh swamped by the incessant questioning of the hundreds who went over the junk." Of course, members of the city's considerable Chinese population were particularly excited and ". . . flocked in great numbers to see the *Amoy*, this link with home making a strong impression on them." The *Colonist* also noted that Captain George Waard's wife, Chang Lee, ". . . garbed in the traditional trousers of her native China, officiated as gatekeeper, [and was] taking toll in the sum of 25 cents of all who passed her."

Long-time *Colonist* contributor Archie Wills, in a story to the paper's weekend supplement, the *Islander*, in May 1970, recalled being on hand for the momentous occasion and meeting Waard, his wife and son, Bobbie, in person. Wills noted that Waard was a rugged seaman who sailed out of Victoria with the sealing fleet in its heyday and then fished on the Fraser River for years. It was there he met Chang Lee, whom he married in Steveston in 1913. That same year the Waards sailed to China where Waard worked for seven years on the Yangtze River as a pilot, followed by a job in the port of Amoy supervising construction of a government dock. Eventually he got homesick for British Columbia and late in 1921 talked his wife into helping him build a junk to sail across the Pacific.

Chinese labour was cheap and plentiful so Waard was able to make good progress getting the vessel ready prior to the April 1922 typhoon season. Still, the three Chinese seamen who signed on as crew—Chan Tai and the brothers Loo and Wong Fook—were quite dismayed when they arrived at the boat to discover it had no eyes and therefore wouldn't be able to "see" on a long voyage. After Waard had fashioned a pair of eyes, 16 inches in diameter, out of camphor wood, a "jossman" (probably Buddhist monk) performed a ceremony and prayed to the appropriate spirits before the eyes were nailed to the *Amoy*, 15 feet back from the bow.

When Captain Waard of the *Amoy* suggested to Percy Shadforth, captain of the pilot boat that came out to meet them, that he might as well tie up at the Outer Harbour, Shadforth said, "No, let's give them a show, we'll sail her right into the Inner Harbour and tie up at The Empress' steps." Note the CPR coastal steamers in the background. VANCOUVER MARITIME MUSEUM PRS10

The junk with seven aboard (a Shanghai River policeman, George Kavalchuck, also joined the crew) cast off on May 17, 1922, for their first port of call, Shanghai. Early one morning, while they were travelling on the river, a python slithered aboard to be quickly dispatched by Captain Waard's revolver. The Chinese crew dined on its meat, and the skin of the python, ". . . which was eleven feet long and as thick as a man's calf," later proved to be of great interest to visitors upon the *Amoy*'s arrival in Victoria Harbour.

The junk spent 10 days in Shanghai and then set off to cross the Sea of Japan where the small craft encountered water spouts and a typhoon and had her rudder fouled by a large fishing net. Arriving in Hakodate, Japan, on July 12, water tanks were filled and charts for the Aleutians secured. Waard's intention was to work the *Amoy* up to the 42nd or 43rd north parallel and hold a course for 30 days for the Juan de Fuca Strait.

The *Amoy* crossed the 180th meridian on August 6 but, after running into a bad southwester with a cross sea, lost her rudder. Captain Waard jury-rigged a replacement and, despite lacking a chart of the area, chanced a run into Nazan Bay in the Aleutian Islands where he had a new rudder installed. Upon leaving, another bad storm was encountered and the replacement rudder gave out under the strain. Not to be deterred, Captain Waard hauled the remains aboard and re-rigged the tiller using tackles from each quarter.

This arrangement held up for the remainder of the voyage and Waard was relieved when Cape Beale light was finally spotted on the west coast of Vancouver Island. After berthing in front of The Empress

The junk *Amoy* garnered a tremendous amount of attention when she moored in front of Victoria's Empress Hotel in September, 1922. The BC Parliament buildings can be seen in the background. MARITIME MUSEUM OF BRITISH COLUMBIA 999.043.0001

Hotel, the final entry in the logbook read, "Arrived Victoria, B.C., noon September 19th 1922, one hundred and twenty-four days from Amoy, China. All's well."

Once in Victoria the Chinese crew of *Amoy* returned to China on the *Empress of Australia*. The Waards, hopeful that stopping at various ports and hosting tours would continue to prove profitable, had the *Amoy* call in at Vancouver, Seattle and Portland on her way to California. After a long stay in San Francisco the junk then continued on to Los Angeles, the West Indies and South America. Captain Waard finally took the *Amoy* up the US eastern seaboard to Bridgeport, Connecticut, where he sold her to a crewman he'd picked up in San Francisco and who in turn sailed her for 20 more years. The last report of the junk *Amoy* has it that she sank in North Carolina's Pimlico Sound in the 1960s.

Captain Waard and Chang Lee returned to BC but unfortunately they drowned in a boating accident off Galiano Island in 1950. Their son, Robert, was living in Vancouver at the time.

### The *Tai Ping*

The *Amoy* wasn't the only oriental vessel to sail across the Pacific in the first half of the last century—there were at least 10, if not more, that arrived in American and Canadian ports up and down the coast. Even though he was only a young boy at the time, Campbell River resident Bob Logan can still vividly recall the day in October 1939 when a Chinese junk appeared in the harbour of his hometown of Ocean Falls. Of

The *Tai Ping* was towed off the rocks at Princess Royal Island by the Balmer Brothers' (managers of the marine shop for Pacific Mills Ltd., Ocean Falls) old cruiser *Charles Todd* and taken into Ocean Falls, but while being lifted onto a scow she slipped off and sank. This photo shows the junk just after being raised from the bottom. BOB LOGAN COLLECTION

course, the arrival of an exotic boat from the far side of the Pacific caused a lot of excitement among the population of the isolated pulp- and paper-mill town, located far up Dean Channel on British Columbia's Central Coast.

The strange and ungainly looking sailing vessel (at least to western eyes) was the small, 50-foot-long *Tai Ping* (Great Peace), which had just completed a 113-day voyage of 5,000 miles across the Pacific from China. Much to Logan's delight and amazement, the stranded American captain and his beautiful wife—who appeared to have stepped right out of a 1930s Hollywood movie—were invited to stay with his grandparents.

Captain John Anderson was working as a Yangtze River pilot based in Shanghai when he realized he and his wife, Nellie, ". . . a White Russian educated in a French convent, who spoke English fluently with an attractive accent . . ." desperately needed to escape from the belligerent Japanese forces that had overrun China. Well familiar with the sailing capabilities of the versatile junks that plied the Yangtze River, he purchased one from its Chinese owner and prepared for a perilous voyage across the Pacific to San Francisco.

However, *Tai Ping* was beset by difficulties and delays right from the start. As soon as they departed, the semi-diesel engine gave out and they were forced to rely on their sails. Then, when the junk stopped in Kobe, Japan, for repairs, her Chinese crew, overcome with seasickness, deserted the vessel. Fortunately

Anderson was able to replace the crew with four European sailors—Hans Liblow, Bergen Larson, Harry Olsen and Charles Kraigh. Unfortunately he was forced to sell his sextant to complete the engine repairs and top up the lockers with fresh provisions.

Finally, on June 14, 1939, *Tai Ping* set sail from Japan only to encounter foul weather and adverse winds for the remainder of the voyage across the Pacific. Some of Danish crewman Charles Kraigh's description of the voyage would later appear in an article in the *Victoria Daily Colonist* on February 11, 1951: ". . . [conditions] did prove the toughest in his 14 years of sailing. Adverse winds, and strong, from east and southeast instead of the westerlies which generally prevail in the latitude the skipper of the junk selected as the course (the route followed by trans-Pacific steamers to and from Japan) helped to upset all calculations. For three weeks after the junk left Kobe gale after gale buffeted *Tai Ping*. Then came a break of 17 days when winds held fair, but bad weather set in again and for 87 days of the 113 days it took to raise the northwest end of Vancouver Island, the junk was constantly battered by stiff winds . . ."

One hundred days later, when they were down to their last drop of water and nearly out of provisions and cigarettes, they sighted the Queen Charlotte Islands, but their troubles weren't over yet. As it happened, the United States survey vessel *Discoverer* came upon the *Tai Ping* flying distress signals off Cape Cook on the exposed northwest coast of Vancouver Island and took her under tow, but the rough seas sprang the foremast and Anderson was forced to cut the junk loose. Then the tiller was carried away, requiring the crew to jury-rig an anchor stock as a replacement. Fortunately the fishing vessel *Flying Cloud*

encountered the junk and took her under tow into Quatsino Sound, northern Vancouver Island. After the stranded crew were supplied with fresh provisions and the damaged craft was repaired, Anderson attempted to make sail for Seattle, but barely 20 miles past Cape Cook *Tai Ping* ran into a howling gale that drove her steadily northwards until she ran up on rocks in Hecate Straits near Princess Royal Island.

The survivors made it to the beach where they were picked up a few days later by a passing fish packer that took them into Ocean Falls. Arrangements were made to tow the *Tai Ping* into the mill town but once there, and while being loaded onto a scow for transportation south, she slipped off the scow and sank in 125 feet of water. When raised, the junk was found to be in such a poor state she was abandoned on a local beach where her remains probably lie to this day.

Captain John Anderson and Nellie were eventually able to make it to Seattle. During the war Anderson got a job as a foreman and assistant to the superintendent at Todd-Seattle Drydocks while he and his wife raised a family. In October 1949 their 12-year-old daughter Angelina (who had been

A rather gaunt Captain John Anderson and his wife, Nellie, are seen here on an Ocean Falls boardwalk in October 1939, following their harrowing voyage across the North Pacific. BOB LOGAN COLLECTION

left behind in China at the age of two and had lived with her maternal grandparents until taken by the Japanese and imprisoned in the Lunghua prison camp in Shanghai for two years) was finally reunited with her parents and two younger sisters.

This is probably Nellie Anderson, wife of Captain John Anderson, trying on a hard hat dive suit, much to the amusement of onlookers aboard the harbour tug *Kwatna*. BOB LOGAN COLLECTION

Captain John Anderson is shown here with the well-known Vancouver hard hat diver Charles Anstee, who worked on raising *Tai Ping* from the bottom at Ocean Falls. Fred Rogers, the retired shipwreck expert, was told by some old mariners that Charles Anstee lost his life later at Prince Rupert while working on anti-submarine nets protecting the harbour. BOB LOGAN COLLECTION

# Chapter 12

# *Drumrock*: Mighty Log Barge was Cape Horn Windjammer, 1927

On February 8, 1927, Pacific (Coyle) Navigation Company contacted the Commissioner of Wrecks in Victoria, BC, to inform them that, "Our barge *Drumrock*, in tow of tug *Pacific Monarch*, became a total loss through stranding in Takush Harbour, Smith Inlet on February 1."

The big steam tug *Pacific Monarch* (ex-*Dreadful*) had headed out from Buckley Bay in Masset Inlet, Queen Charlotte Islands, on January 29 making its way south to Squirrel Cove at Cortez Island with the log barge *Drumrock* on the towline loaded with some 950,000 board feet of hemlock and spruce logs. Tug and tow never made it intact across Queen Charlotte Sound.

*Pacific Monarch* was bucking into a southeast gale with 40-knot winds as she attempted to cross the Sound and, at 10:30 a.m. on February 1, the long-time Pacific (Coyle) skipper, Captain Hugh Stanley McLellan, apparently decided he'd had enough, turned around and headed for shelter. At 3:45 p.m., with tug and barge safely in Takush Harbour, Captain McLellan was attempting to anchor his tow when the deeply laden barge hung up on an uncharted rock and stranded. On board the log barge at the time were the barge master, John P. Johnson, and 10 bargees.

The massive Pacific (Coyle) Navigation log carrier, originally launched as the steel Cape Horn windjammer *Drumrock*, was 329 feet in length and 3,182 gross tonnage. She was built as a four-masted barque in 1891 in Leith, Scotland, by Ramage & Ferguson for the Liverpool shipping interests, Gillison & Chadwick. *Drumrock* sailed under the British merchant fleet's "red duster" until 1899 and was then sold to Reederai F. Laeisz of Hamburg, Germany. The massive square-rigger was renamed *Persimmon* and joined that company's famous Flying "P" line of sailing ships, which were heavily involved in the nitrate trade from Chile around Cape Horn. Nitrates mined in the high desert of Chile were valued as a necessary ingredient for both fertilizer and gunpowder in Europe.

Sometime around 1913 *Persimmon* was sold to another German shipping firm, F.A. Vinnen & Company of Bremen, and renamed *Helwig Vinnen*. In the spring of 1914 she was on her way down the Elbe River with her holds filled with German coke destined for a copper smelter at Santa Rosalia, Baja, California. *Helwig Vinnen* arrived in the Mexican port on the last day of August only to find herself interned for the remainder of the First World War, which had broken out in Europe earlier that month.

The German master and crew of *Helwig Vinnen* had plenty of company since 11 other full-rigged ships and four-masted barques from their country were also trapped in Santa Rosalia, where their decks blistered in the desert-like heat for seven years. Finally, in 1923, San Francisco lumberman Robert Dollar bought all

The majestic four-masted steel barque *Drumrock* is pictured here, probably riding at anchor, at Semaphore Anchorage, Port Adelaide, Australia. COURTESY OF STATE LIBRARY OF SOUTH AUSTRALIA PRG1273/6/49

12 Cape Horn windjammers from the various Allied countries that had been awarded them by the Allied Reparations Commission. Dollar was hoping to regain his position in the trans-Pacific trade to the Orient by utilizing sailing ships to transport his lumber products. He had had a sizable fleet of steamships prior to the war but had sold all to aid the war effort.

When *Helwig Vinnen* was found to be unsuitable, Dollar put her up for sale and the derelict square-rigger was subsequently bought by Hecate Straits Towing Company of Vancouver, BC, and was towed out of San Francisco Bay in early January 1925. Four other of Dollar's German windjammers were also destined to end up in British Columbia where they were cut down into barges: *Harvestehude* (ex-*Riversdale*); *Adolph Vinnen*; *Orotava (ex-Comet)*; and *Walküre*.

In October 1925 the *BC Lumberman* ran a feature story on the new log-carrying barge *Drumrock*. It reported that the managing owners of Hecate Straits Towing Company, Messrs. Johnson, Walton & Company of Vancouver, had completed the conversion of the former four-masted steel barque *Helwig Vinnen*. Only the year before, British Pacific Transport Co. Ltd., also of Vancouver, had had the very first self-loading and unloading log barge built by using the undocumented wooden hull of the American-built Ferris freighter *Bingamon*. After a bad experience in January 1925, in which the barge was almost lost on her first voyage to the Queen Charlotte Islands, it was decided steel or iron hulls would probably prove more durable.

In 1925, the *Drumrock* was converted to a self-loading and unloading log barge. The massive 329-foot, Scottish-built, riveted steel hull proved ideal for hauling logs across the treacherous waters of Hecate Straits and Queen Charlotte Sound. VANCOUVER MARITIME MUSEUM

Each of *Drumrock*'s three hatches had five winches that were controlled by one operator stationed 10 feet above the main deck. "All the control gear is very conveniently assembled and easy to operate. A powerful brake is attached to each winch, while all the steelwork has been built with a test of 30 tons and a guaranteed faction of eight tons."—*BC Lumberman*. VANCOUVER MARITIME MUSEUM, 5629

Concerned with possible hold-ups and problems with the established shipyards, Barney Johnson leased the Terminal City Dock, hired his own workforce and assembled the necessary riveting, cutting and other required equipment. During the conversion, the barque's lower yards were turned into 60-ton (capacity) derricks, and five winches (tapping, loading and yarding winches and two swinging winches) were installed alongside each of the three 58-foot x 36-foot hatches. With her original name reinstated, *BC Lumberman* concluded, "The *Drumrock* will carry 1,000,000 board feet of logs each trip . . . from the Queen Charlotte Islands to Vancouver in four days in place of the 15 days required for boom-towing. The crew will consist of 13 or 14 men, including loaders, winch-men and drivers. A unique feature of the equipment of the *Drumrock* is a low-tower (power) radiophone, which is installed in the pilothouse to enable the ship to keep in constant communication with tug ahead."

After a sizable financial outlay for the innovative design, the log barge *Drumrock* saw barely a year's service before she was lost to this marine mishap in Smith Inlet. When she stranded in February 1927, *Drumrock* was drawing some 22 feet of water with her massive load. The tide was falling and at low water, at 7:00 p.m. that evening, *Drumrock* broke in two. The "Return for Wreck Register," the official record of the stranding, noted, "Accident could not have been avoided. Barge total loss, cargo intact." In his final report to the Commissioner of Wrecks in Ottawa the Deputy to the Commissioner concluded that those on board both the log carrier and tug *Pacific Monarch* ". . . can be in no sense held to blame."

Longtime UASBC member David Stone explores the former Cape Horn windjammer *Drumrock*—a very attractive shallow water dive in Takush Harbour, Smith Inlet. The sheer size of the ship with her classic sailing ship prow and bowsprit make this one of the most attractive underwater heritage sites anywhere on BC's Central Coast.

JACQUES MARC PHOTO

# Chapter 13

# The Wrecks of Wreck Beach, 1928

While Wreck Beach near Point Grey continues to be a popular recreation spot for Vancouver residents—especially since the wearing of clothing remains optional—few who frequent it have any idea how the site may have earned its name. There was indeed a shipwreck off the beach in the early 1920s, but it was only a small vessel that left too little in the way of wreckage for it to garner much attention, let alone have a piece of geography named for the incident. What may have been the wrecks of Wreck Beach didn't arrive until sometime in the late 1920s and they actually weren't wrecks at all. Instead they were some old hulks that were intentionally sunk there for use as a breakwater.

The only recorded loss of a vessel was that of the coastal freighter *Trader* (101 feet in length and 172

The remains of one of the many Ferris hull wood cargo steamers built in the US during World War I is scuttled at Wreck Beach. D.M. THOMSON COLLECTION, VANCOUVER MARITIME MUSEUM

tons gross) off the North Arm jetty in the spring of 1923. The small steamer's first owner was the Gulf Steamship and Trading Company Ltd. of Victoria, who used her on a freight run to and from Puget Sound. While in that service, carrying a cargo of canned salmon, she happened to collide with the sternwheeler *Capital City* near Tacoma in 1902. *Trader* was transferred to the Trader Steamship Company Ltd., also of Victoria, around 1919, and the rest of her career was devoted to the workaday role of carrying freight and passengers throughout the Strait of Georgia as well as to remote northern logging camps.

On March 16, 1923, *Trader* was headed into Vancouver with a cargo of cement from Vancouver Island when she ran into heavy weather as she tried to round Point Grey. In an attempt to run for cover, Captain Fred Anderson pointed her bow for the safety of the Fraser River. Unfortunately, the gale drove her up onto a sandbar just 200 yards from the North Arm jetty.

The crew could do nothing for her in the falling tide so they took the lifeboat to shore. By the time the storm abated, *Trader* had taken a pounding. The hull was holed and her upperworks were smashed, and as a result she was written off as a complete loss.

*Trader's* boiler and engines were later salvaged and the hull was moved to a beach across the river. There she was abandoned, and for many years *Trader's* half-buried wooden skeleton, filled with sacks of solidified cement, could be seen along Wreck Beach. Today the wreck is no longer visible but the shifting sands may uncover her remains sometime in the future.

The other "wrecks" of Wreck Beach were far more substantial than *Trader* and it was these vessels that probably provided the inspiration for the name. In January 1950, Vancouver City archivist Major J.S. Matthews placed a query in local newspapers asking if anyone knew how Wreck Beach got its name. Two months later Matthews published an article titled "Mystery Name Solved" detailing what he'd learned. According to replies to his query, three wood log barges (the Ferris hulls *Biscayne*, *Bingamon* and *Black Wolf*) and a floating grain elevator (*Blatchford*) were towed around the North Arm in 1928 to act as a breakwater for the log storage grounds. A steel ore carrier, *Granco*, was also supposedly added to the collection.

While Major Matthews' sources were correct about *Bingamon* and *Granco* being part of the breakwater site, the other names suggested are probably wrong. *Biscayne* foundered as a Pacific (Coyle) log barge off Cape Beale in 1932; *Black Wolf*, a log barge in the same fleet, stranded in 1929 in Skidegate Inlet, Queen Charlotte Islands, where she lies on the bottom to this day; and the former floating grain elevator *Blatchford* joined a collection of floating breakwater hulks at Powell River around 1936.

When he was researching his detailed history of British Columbia's early log barges, which was published in *Sea Chest: The Journal of the Puget Sound Maritime Historical Society* in 2001, maritime historian Frank Clapp interviewed Captain Joseph S. Marston of Victoria and Ernest Taylor of Ladner, both of whom, as boys, had lived near today's Wreck Beach. Both of them seemed quite certain four hulks were laid to rest there. The most likely Ferris hulls to have accompanied *Bingamon* are *Chalcis* and *Abydos*, originally owned by the British Pacific Transport Company but never put into service as barges. Another possibility is the Pacific (Coyle) Navigation Company log barge *Abnoba*, which sank in Nootka Sound in 1929 and was later raised and towed to Vancouver.

In the late 1920s, Pacific (Coyle) Navigation was leasing booming grounds along the North Arm of the Fraser River and federal records indicate that the firm's subsidiary, Burrard Boom Company, submitted plans to the Department of Public Works for the construction of a close-pile wall to shelter the grounds. Once they realized how expensive this undertaking was going to be, they resorted to scuttling old hulks as breakwaters instead.

Here, *Bingamon* is pictured with her massive loading crane on rails. On *Bingamon*'s maiden voyage as a log barge in January 1925, while under tow of the tug *Masset* crossing Queen Charlotte Sound in a howling gale, it was this crane that wreaked havoc when it broke loose. VANCOUVER PUBLIC LIBRARY, SPECIAL COLLECTIONS VPL 21910

On October 24, 1928, the *Victoria Daily Colonist* reported that the self-loading log barge *Bingamon* was to be towed to the North Arm of the Fraser River and sunk as a breakwater. Six days later, Pacific (Coyle) Navigation's tug *Cape Scott* performed the task. Another hulk, *Granco,* apparently followed shortly afterward, since Pacific (Coyle) finally registered the hulk on January 17, 1930, possibly to ensure that it was recognized as private property and not an abandoned derelict on the beach.

*Bingamon* was a unique vessel with a very interesting history. She began life as one of some 161 Ferris-type wooden freighters built in Washington and Oregon state shipyards for the United States Shipping Board during the First World War. These 265- to 268-foot-long steamships of some 2,200 to 2,500 gross tons were a single deck with a "three-island" superstructure design. The *Bingamon*, United States Emergency Fleet Corporation (EFC) Contract 94, was launched from the Sanderson & Porter shipyard in Raymond, Washington, on January 14, 1919. However, *Bingamon*, like many of the American-built freighters built late during the Great War, never served in her intended role since the war was over before she could be completed.

By the end of 1918 (the Armistice was signed on November 11, 1918) the EFC had taken delivery of only 118 of 589 wood freighters built in various shipyards throughout the United States. Only 87 of these saw more than a month of service while the rest saw none whatsoever. A post-war depression accompanied a peacetime oversupply of shipping and the resulting depressed freight rates saw the bulk of the US ship-building program rafted together in backwaters such as Lake Union, Washington, where a derelict fleet of some 40 hulls became known as "Wilson's Woodrow" (Woodrow Wilson was US President during the First World War). *Bingamon* happened to be one of 10 unused Washington-built Ferris-type hulls that ended up being purchased in the early 1920s for use in British Columbia waters as log barges. (*Abnoba, Abydos, Bingamon, Blatchford, Biscayne, Black Wolf* and *Chalcis* were all examples of the Ferris design.)

In December 1924, the British Pacific Log Transport Company, Ltd. bought *Bingamon* from Washington Tug & Barge, who had purchased 23 Ferris-type hulls from the United States Shipping Board. British Pacific then set to work converting her into the West Coast's first self-loading log barge. Up until this time the Davis raft was the preferred choice for transporting logs from coastal logging operations to lumber mills, but the loss of logs while towing them in rafts, especially across open waters such as the treacherous Hecate Straits, was heavy, resulting in costly insurance rates. It was hoped that by using derelict ships for barges, logs would be delivered safely, quickly and at less cost, and that the wood would also be less susceptible to marine borers.

Unfortunately, the innovative vessel was almost lost on her first voyage, to the Queen Charlotte Islands in early January 1925. Norman Hacking, who wrote the column "Ship and Shore" for the *Vancouver Province* in the 1960s, recalled talking with Bill Ballantyne, who was engineer on the big steam tug *Masset* for *Bingamon's* trial run. *Bingamon*, while under tow of *Masset*, was halfway across Queen Charlotte Sound in a big blow when the six bargees (barge crew) sent up a distress signal. The massive crane had broken loose and was careering out of control up and down the rails, creating chaos aboard the vessel. The tug managed to get the barge in her lee, allowing the crane to be secured, but it wasn't over yet.

On the way across Hecate Straits, in the midst of the raging gale, *Masset's* 50-ton water tank burst, flooding the engine room. Coal, water and ashes rose to within two inches of the boiler furnaces. With no option but to run before the wind, tug and tow were driven toward Prince Rupert. Finally, off Triple Island, the towline parted and *Bingamon* disappeared with her six bargees aboard. Fortunately she drifted into a rocky bay where they were able to anchor their vessel safely in sheltered waters. Once a new towline could be attached, tug and barge headed across to the Queen Charlotte Islands once again and when they reached Cumshewa Inlet nearly a million board feet of prime spruce logs were loaded aboard *Bingamon*. As Hacking has it, as the last log was put in place the crane collapsed in pieces.

The British Pacific Transport Company's hulks mothballed at Bedwell Bay, located up Indian Arm in Burrard Inlet, in November 1928, are identified as (left to right) *Addison, Abydos, Endymion, Chalcis, Abnoba* and *Oelwein*, along with Pacific (Coyle) Navigation's steel-hulled *Granco*. VANCOUVER MARITIME MUSEUM

Regardless of this unfortunate start, *Bingamon* soon proved a success and, with the need for more log barges by the forest industry, the British Pacific Log Transport Company (the name was changed to British Pacific Barge Company, Ltd. in August 1925) had nine more Ferris hulls towed up from Lake Union to Vancouver that summer and moored them in Bedwell Bay, Indian Arm, in readiness for conversion.

*Bingamon* herself had only seen about three and a half years of barge service when, on July 7, 1928, she caught fire while anchored in Plumper Harbour, Nootka Sound. Some 90 feet of her stern were burned to the water's edge and her hoisting machinery was ruined. *Bingamon* was towed to Esquimalt where she subsequently sank in the harbour. Once refloated, she was written off as a total loss. The *Victoria Daily Colonist* of October 26 reported, "The log carrier *Bingamon*, now merely a shell with part of her stern levelled off, is being patched with canvas in the drydock for towing to the Fraser River . . ." Soon afterward, she was finally laid to rest on the mud flats off Wreck Beach.

Like *Bingamon*, the hulk *Granco* had had a varied and unusual past. She was originally launched as the 275-foot-long, 2,114-net-ton steamship *Barracouta* from the shipyard of J. & G. Thompson in Glasgow, Scotland, in 1883. She was first owned by the Barracouta S.S. Co. and was registered in London. *The Record of American and Foreign Shipping* noted that she was regularly surveyed in New York from 1883 through to 1888, implying she probably served on a trans-Atlantic steamship run. In 1893 she was surveyed in San Francisco and four years later was acquired by the Pacific Mail Steamship Company. *Barracouta* operated as part of their Panama fleet out of the port of San Francisco up until 1915 when Pacific Mail terminated service and sold off their steamship fleet.

Sometime between 1915 and 1917, the out-of-service steamer *Barracouta* was purchased by Griffiths & Sons, a major Puget Sound towing company, for conversion into a barge. She was then transferred over to the company's Canadian subsidiary, Coastwise Steamship & Barge Co., and assigned to their regular run transporting ore from northern British Columbia to a smelter in Tacoma, Washington. In early December 1917, the huge barge, encrusted with some six to eight inches of ice, was swept from her anchorage in

In 1897, the *Barracouta* was acquired by the Pacific Mail Steamship Company and operated as part of their fleet out of San Francisco until the service was terminated in 1915. Since it is dated 1915, this photo may have been taken following her last voyage with the company. SAN FRANCISCO MARITIME NATIONAL HISTORICAL PARK, B7.1,902PL

Seward, Alaska, and carried away by a gale. Since she didn't look very different from an iceberg, the *San Francisco Chronicle* reported, ". . . searchers passed her by many times." Eventually the huge barge was located with the three crew members still safe aboard.

Apparently *Barracouta* underwent a name change while with Coastwise Steamship & Barge, since the 1920–21 Lloyd's Register lists her as "*Granco*, steel barge, former S.S. *Baracouta* [*sic*]" for the first time. In February 1927, Coastwise Steamship Company sold off their ore carrier to Albert & McCaffery Ltd., a Prince Rupert building supply company who, a month later, turned around and sold *Granco* to Pacific (Coyle) Navigation Company, who brought her to join *Bingamon* on Wreck Beach.

One of Major Matthews' informants told him in 1950 that, while there were originally four hulks at Wreck Beach, only the remains of two were left. He went on to say that the wood vessel (probably *Bingamon*) was set afire back in the "Hungry '30s" in order to salvage scrap metal for sale.

According to a 1943 file on the *Granco* in the National Archives in Ottawa, Wartime Salvage Ltd. intended to have her broken up on site for some 1,000 to 1,500 tons of much needed steel for the war effort in late 1942. However, the plan to remove the hulk met with heavy opposition from the North Fraser Harbour Commission since ". . . the barge, plus a wooden hulk, forms an indispensable part of the protection southward from Point Grey behind which log booming areas have been constructed." The file doesn't indicate what became of *Granco* but what is certain is that her remains haven't been visible for decades.

This is probably the remains of the *Granco* at Wreck Beach. The steel barge was originally launched as the trans-Atlantic steamship *Barracouta*. Griffiths & Sons, a major Puget Sound towing company, transferred her to their Canadian subsidiary, Coastwise Steamship & Barge Company, sometime around 1915 to 1917 for use as a barge transporting ore from northern BC mines to a Tacoma smelter. D.M. THOMSON COLLECTION, VANCOUVER MARITIME MUSEUM

# Chapter 14

# Island Tug & Barge Gave Old Sailers Second Wind, 1937

"Better to be taken care of and wind up their affairs in gainful occupation than be transformed into scrap before their days of usefulness are done," Harold Elworthy, manager of Island Tug & Barge Ltd., remarked to a Victoria *Times Colonist* reporter in April of 1937.

Victoria's Inner Harbour towing firm had just bought the five-masted barquentine *Forest Friend*, which had been lying idle up the Fraser River since 1929, to cut down into a barge. *Forest Friend*, launched in Aberdeen, Washington, in 1919, became part of a fleet that eventually included 13 retired sailing vessels that Island Tug & Barge purchased for their cheap bottoms to haul wood chips, hog fuel (scrap wood waste from sawmills used to fire boilers in pulp and paper mills) and, following the Second World War, logs.

Advances in the mechanics of steam propulsion in the late nineteenth century foreshadowed the demise of the wind-driven vessel. By the 1930s a large sailing vessel seen off the Victoria waterfront was a special occasion as few were left in active service, although old-timers could recall when it was a daily occurrence to see ships powered by billowing white canvas entering Juan de Fuca Strait looking for a tow to a Puget Sound or British Columbia port. A few of these tall-masted ships, however, gained a reprieve from the wreckers. Shorn of their tall spars, with hatchways opened up and some of their main and 'tween decks ripped out, once graceful wooden lumber schooners and barquentines, along with massive Cape Horn square-riggers, were converted into utilitarian barges.

Harold Elworthy's Island Tug & Barge started operations in 1925 by towing a boom of logs with the small tug *Island Planet* for the grand sum of $125. From this modest start, the company went on to develop a substantial fleet of towboats and barges that hauled forest products throughout British Columbia and Washington state, but the local Victoria company wasn't the first on the West Coast to introduce the practice of converting retired ships into barges. An earlier entrepreneur in northwest Pacific coast towing, James Griffiths & Sons based in Puget Sound, began the practice around the turn of the twentieth century. Deepwater square-riggers bought at low prices and transformed into barges helped build Griffiths' fortune. *Melanope* (see Chapter 6) was one of these ships.

Gordon Gibson, of early west coast Vancouver Island logging fame, claimed the distinction of developing the first self-powered, self-loading and unloading log barge. In 1934 the rough and tumble Gibson Brothers outfit purchased the 1,550-ton wood-hulled *Malahat* and fitted her with two steam donkeys for loading logs.

A sister ship of *Laurel Whalen*, built by Cameron-Genoa Mills Shipbuilders Ltd. of Victoria in 1917,

Harold Elworthy restricted Island Tug & Barge Company's wood-hulled sailing ship barges to carrying hog fuel and wood chips and had them avoid open waters as much as possible. The *Betsey Ross* (shown here loading hog fuel), *Drumwall*, *Sir Thomas J. Lipton* and *Forest Friend* plied between lumber mills on Vancouver Island and pulp and paper mills in Washington State. HAROLD ELWORTHY COLLECTION

*Malahat* was originally launched as a deepwater lumber freighter, but the five-masted auxiliary schooner was retired from the trade in 1922. *Malahat* then became involved in a profitable trade as a floating warehouse and mother ship to the rum-running fleet off the coast of California and Mexico. After the end of Prohibition in the United States in 1933, *Malahat* was picked up by the Gibsons who didn't bother to re-register her as a freight ship. Under load, the auxiliary power of the two old Swedish Bolinder semi-diesel engines could barely manage in rough weather in the confined waters of BC's coast, and after courting disaster once too often *Malahat* was relegated to the towline.

Art Elworthy, one of Harold's sons, recalled that the company restricted their old wood-hulled sailing vessels to carrying wood chips and hog fuel and had them avoid open water as much as possible. The former barquentines *Forest Friend* and *Drumwall* (ex-*Puako*), along with the schooners *Sir Thomas J. Lipton* and *Betsey Ross*, plied between the BC lumber mills in Port Alberni and Chemainus and the ports of Port Townsend and Port Angeles in Washington state.

Many of these ex-sailing vessels were given new names more suited to their drab roles as barges (see below). The four-masted barquentine *Puako*, for example, whose Hawaiian name meant "flower of the sugar cane," was renamed *Drumwall* by Hecate Straits Towing Co. who purchased her in 1925 and cut her down into a barge. She was subsequently sold to Island Tug & Barge.

The four-masted steel barque *Comet* served her barge years with Island Tug & Barge under the utilitarian

*Melanope* is pictured here as a cut-down CPR collier passing through Vancouver's First Narrows with a full load aboard. Note the crane amidships for discharging coal into CPR Empress liners. H. BROWN PHOTO, JULY 1925, COURTESY ROYAL BC MUSEUM, BC ARCHIVES A-07611

## Names and Origins

| Island Tug & Barge Company's Sailing Ship Barges | Barge Launched As |
|---|---|
| *Homeward Bound* | steel ship *Zemindar*, Belfast, Ireland, 1885 |
| *Lord Templetown* | steel barque *Lord Templetown*, Belfast, 1886 |
| *Dunsyre* | steel ship *Dunsyre*, Port Glasgow, Scotland, 1891 |
| *Island Forester* | steel barque *Comet*, Port Glasgow, 1901 |
| *Fibreboard* | steel barque *Robert Duncan*, Port Glasgow, 1892 |
| *Island Carrier* | steel barque *Somali*, Port Glasgow, 1892 |
| *Island Star* | steel ship *Blairmore*, Dumbarton, Scotland, 1893 |
| *Riversdale* | steel ship *Riversdale*, Port Glasgow, 1894 |
| *Drumwall* | wood, four-masted barquentine *Puako*, Oakland, Ca., 1902 |
| *Island Gatherer* | steel barque *Alsterberg*, Dumbarton, 1902 |
| *Betsey Ross* | wood five-masted schooner *Betsy Ross*, Tacoma, Wa., 1917 (*"Betsey"* was probably an I.T.& B. Co. misspelling) |
| *Forest Friend* | wood five-masted barquentine *Forest Friend*, Aberdeen, Wa., 1919 |
| *Sir Thomas J. Lipton* | wood four-masted schooner *Sir Thomas J. Lipton* Brunswick, Georgia, 1919 |

The log barge *Island Forester,* riding light and high out of the water with the tug *Island Navigator* alongside, dominates Victoria's Upper Harbour. The photo was probably taken soon after the end of the Second World War since the log barge is still in reasonable shape and has yet to have her loading cranes installed. (*Island Navigator* was one of a number of Mikimiki tugs built in the US during the war and then sold off with the return of peace.)
MARITIME MUSEUM OF BRITISH COLUMBIA P 1181.06

name *Island Forester. Somali,* at one time one of the largest commercial sailing ships afloat under the British flag at 3,410 gross tons and 330 feet in length, became *Island Carrier.*

The steel three-masted ship *Riversdale,* the schooner *Thomas J. Lipton,* the steel ship *Dunsyre* and the stately barque *Lord Templetown* all retained their original names while in service with the Elworthy fleet. When the old windjammers *Somali, Comet, Riversdale* and *Blairmore* were sold by Island Tug & Barge Co. to Crown Zellerbach in the mid-1950s their new names gave no clue as to their former, more dignified careers, their only identification being *Crown Zellerbach #1, #2, #3* and *#4* painted on their counters.

Most of the coast's old sailing ships whose lives were extended by barge conversion have long since disappeared. Of those who worked under the Island Tug & Barge Co. flag *Lord Templetown, Blairmore* (barge *Island Star*) and *Zemindar* (barge *Homeward Bound*) went to the Capital Iron Co. breaker yard in Victoria Harbour. In the winter gales of 1936 both *Dunsyre* (while still under canvas, the first sailing ship through the Panama Canal) and *Island Gatherer* were lost in marine mishaps (see Chapter 15). Fortunately, in both instances, the "bargees" (the barge crew of usually three men responsible for steering the ship, slipping the lines, picking up tow, etc.) managed to escape with their lives. A few hulks did manage to escape the cutting torch and avoid disaster along the coast, and the remains of five exist as part of the old hulk breakwater at Royston, a little south of Courtenay on Vancouver Island (see Chapter 17). The prominent bow of *Riversdale* is lodged in the rock ballast with the bow of the *Comet* fallen over to seaward. There,

After the Second World War, three large steam cranes were installed on the *Island Forester* for self-loading and unloading logs. Here the size of the logs, probably spruce butt ends, suggests the barge is probably loading in the Queen Charlotte Islands. HAROLD ELWORTHY COLLECTION

too, rest *Forest Friend* and *Laurel Whalen*, as well as the collier *Melanope*. Disappearing into the mud nearby are two of her old towboats, the CPR's steam tugs *Nanoose* and *Qualicum*. Ships bells, wheels, figureheads, and brass fittings salvaged from these vessels are scattered throughout museums and private homes along the West Coast. The large wooden wheel of *Melanope* is displayed in the Maritime Museum of British Columbia in Victoria, while her brass bell hangs in the Comox Legion. Several tons of gear were rescued from *Lord Templetown* before she was scrapped in Portland, Oregon, and sent to the San Francisco Maritime Museum.

In 1970, to aid in the restoration of another Cape Horn windjammer, *Wavertree*, Capital Iron sent a crew to Royston and stripped *Riversdale* of its bollards, fairleads, windlass and capstan. Some enterprising and historically minded Americans had retrieved *Wavertree* from South America and the vessel is now open to public viewing at the South Street Seaport Museum in Manhattan, New York.

In British Columbia, although a few of the former steel square-riggers were still afloat as barges as late as the 1960s, none was saved to remind us of the varied roles they served in our maritime heritage. All that remains is a few broken and collapsed hulks now resting at Royston, slowly succumbing to the elements and disappearing into the Courtenay River's estuary mud.

# Chapter 15

# Adrift in a West Coast Gale:
# The *Dunsyre* and *Island Gatherer*, 1936

The winter of 1936 was a hard one for Victoria's Island Tug & Barge Company. On November 17, the company barge *Dunsyre* went adrift in a raging gale off the west coast of Vancouver Island and was dashed to pieces the next day on Kains Island at the entrance to Quatsino Sound.

A month later, the *Victoria Daily Times* of December 15 reported that another barge, *Island Gatherer,* had also lost its towline during a southeaster. This time, the disaster occurred in the treacherous waters of Queen Charlotte Sound, and after the barge crew was rescued, the hapless vessel was never seen again.

These massive hulks were two of the collection of retired sailing ships that Harold Elworthy, owner of Island Tug & Barge Company, had bought during the Depression for hauling wood chips and hog fuel along the West Coast. Old iron and steel windjammers were ideally suited for this role once they were shorn of their tall spars, their hatchways had been opened and some decking was cut away. When they were stripped down, the after cabin—the captain's inner sanctum—was always left intact. It was here that the barge's captain (possibly a former windjammer master fallen on hard times) lived. As master of the barge he looked after such chores as handling lines and firing up the steam donkey, and he was generally responsible for taking care of the owner's interests while lying in port. He was usually joined by two seamen while under tow.

*Island Gatherer* was one of three already stripped-down hulls that the Victoria towboating entrepreneur bought from Pacific (Coyle) Navigation Company in 1936. Pacific (Coyle) had named her *Pacific Gatherer,* but she started her deep-sea sailing career as *Alsterberg,* a 330-foot, 3,239-ton, steel four-masted barque launched from Dumbarton, Scotland, in 1902. Island Tug had purchased their other recently cut-down windjammer, *Dunsyre,* in 1935 in San Francisco, where she had been laid up since the early 1920s. She had been originally launched in 1891 in Port Glasgow, Scotland, as the *Dunsyre,* a steel three-masted ship of 2,056 tons and 279 feet in length.

Alan Heater, crewing on the tug *Anyox* in November 1936, found himself assigned to the barge *Dunsyre* that ill-fated winter. Still in his teens, Heater had landed a job that fall with Island Tug & Barge after mentioning that he had just spent a summer with his grandfather, Bill Heater, whaling in the North Pacific. Elworthy hired him on the spot.

*Anyox* was returning with the empty *Dunsyre* from the paper mill in Port Alice when the tow was caught in a West Coast gale. The over-stressed hawser parted between the two vessels and *Anyox* frantically tried to rocket a line across to the wallowing hulk in order to rescue Captain W. Billington, Ray Larkin

The three-masted steel ship *Dunsyre*, built in Port Glasgow in 1891, was said to be the first sailing ship to pass through the Panama Canal when it opened in 1914. She is pictured here riding at anchor at an unidentified port.
VANCOUVER MARITIME MUSEUM

and Heater. After two unsuccessful attempts, the third succeeded, but as *Anyox*'s crew was preparing to send across a heavy line and breeches buoy to the barge, the sound of the booming surf informed them that they were dangerously close to the rocky shoreline. As the barge drifted closer to the breakers, Captain F.H. Cole, skipper of *Anyox*, took the decision to abandon the rescue rather than sacrifice his wooden-hull tug with some 15 men aboard.

Left drifting and alone, the three bargees were reluctant to share their thoughts on the inevitable; that when the helpless craft finally hit the rocks they wouldn't stand a chance. "We saw the last of *Anyox* about an hour after dark on Tuesday night, and from that time on were alone with the breaking seas, which did everything possible with the barge except stand her on end. It's a good thing she was riding light and not handicapped with a load . . ." Captain Billington later told a reporter.

To keep their spirits up, Alan Heater drew his mouth organ out of his pocket and played *Home Sweet Home*. Then, around 1:30 in the morning, a large object loomed out of the dark, which Captain Billington identified as Solander Island. Incredibly, *Dunsyre*, drifting stern first in the storm, rather than going up on the island or onto the rocks scattered throughout the water between it and Cape Cook, passed through the passage unscathed.

Billington recalled that, "All through the night, from minute to minute, we just expected to hit bottom. *Dunsyre* rolled heavily from crest to trough and to crest again with monotonous regularity, shipping

In September 1930, *Island Gatherer*, as Pacific (Coyle) Navigation Company's *Pacific Gatherer*, was involved in a bizarre accident. In tow of the tug *Lorne*, the barge was caught in an eddy and swept into the Second Narrows Bridge, lifting a span off with the rising tide. Stories have it that the captain of the *Lorne* committed suicide soon after. VANCOUVER PUBLIC LIBRARY, SPECIAL COLLECTIONS VPL 3115

heavy spray continually as we carried on. We had the lifeboat in slings all ready to swing out on the lee side of the ship, but I'm certain it wouldn't have been of much use if we had gone ashore in the sea that was running."

At dawn's break, the three men decided their only chance of survival was to get away in the lifeboat. The six-foot-tall Heater volunteered to go over the stern in the boat since they all knew he was probably the only one strong enough to hold it off from the crushing force of the rolling barge's counter. The bargees successfully cleared the doomed ship and Heater managed the large tiller while his two mates manned the oars. At first the thick weather and high waves made it impossible to gauge whether the boat was being blown farther out to sea or landward. Then, after three hours of scanning the horizon, they picked out the flashing beacon of Kains Island lighthouse. Their problems weren't over yet, however. The island was surrounded by rocks and reefs that made it a formidable place to land at the best of times.

Here Heater proved his worth as a seaman by threading a safe a passage through the reefs as Captain Billington and Ray Larkin leaned into the oars. Once they were in behind the island they rode in on a big swell, jumped to shore and turned to see the next swell smash the lifeboat into staves. Three hours later the lightkeeper, his wife, the wireless operator and the three survivors all watched as the gale-blown *Dunsyre* was driven broadside onto the rocky island. In less than half an hour only the top of her housework remained to identify the wreck as a once stately square-rigger.

Another teenager, Joe Quilty, was just out of school in the Depression year of 1935 when he approached Harold Elworthy and offered to work for his board to gain some experience. Elworthy told him to be at the company dock at eight the next morning when *Salvage Queen* (the retired CPR coastal steamer *Tees*) was pulling out. December 1936 found the young seaman on the big tug taking the loaded *Island Carrier* to Ocean Falls, to return with the empty *Island Gatherer* through the inside waters of Johnstone Straits.

Quilty was aboard *Island Gatherer* when the tow entered the open waters of the notorious Queen Charlotte Sound. With Bull Harbour station reporting winds of 92 knots that night, the tug and barge found themselves in the midst of a full-blown North Pacific hurricane.

"The crew on the *Salvage Queen* had to turn on the steam winch to hold the towline because the brake was slipping and the line was gradually working off the drum," Quilty recalled. "Then the crank disks on the towing winch snapped in half from the strain . . . the brake wouldn't hold and all the line ran off the drum. *We were adrift!* . . . but with all that towline draggin' more or less kept head into the wind . . . but if we'd been broadside, don't think would have got us off."

Quilty was off watch at the time and when he came on deck to discover *Salvage Queen* gone he feared the worst. He still considers it miraculous that the tug eventually found them. The tug captain, Frederick MacFarlane, had always told his bargees that if they ever went adrift he would get them all off or the towboat would go to the bottom trying. As it was, when MacFarlane brought *Salvage Queen* in close to the massive hulk towering over his wheelhouse, the tug sustained a major amount of damage. As Joe

The *Salvage Queen* was the converted CPR coastal steamer *Tees*, purchased by the Canadian Pacific Navigation Company in 1893 and registered in the name of the CPR in March 1903. She was renamed *Salvage Queen* after being sold to the Pacific Salvage Company in 1925. She is shown here in First Narrows in about 1930, a few years before Island Tug & Barge acquired her. VANCOUVER MARITIME MUSEUM

Quilty described it, the wallowing *Island Gatherer* ". . . smashed the foremast out . . . bust the wheelhouse, smashed the davits in on starboard side, bust lifeboat starboard side and pushed starboard anchor right through the bow . . . so she was takin' a lot of water!"

One crewman was able to jump off on his own but Joe Quilty and Captain Poulson remained behind. Quilty assisted the desperately seasick Mrs. Poulson while Captain Poulson struggled with the barge. (Mrs. Poulson later told local papers that she considered Joe Quilty an "angel" for his actions throughout the ordeal.)

With *Salvage Queen* finally in position, Quilty and Poulson helped Mrs. Poulson along the side of the barge where they sat on a handrail and waited for the right wave. When it arrived, they picked up the elderly woman and unceremoniously tossed her toward the foredeck of the tug, where the waiting crew caught her in a canvas tarp.

Captain Poulson and Quilty then jumped to safety. While Captain MacFarlane had performed a daring rescue with no loss of life, *Salvage King* was wrecked beyond repair by the wallowing *Island Gatherer* in the high seas drama.

Looking back, both Joe Quilty and Alan Heater dismissed any thought of the idea during their 1996 interviews that they were heroes 60 years earlier. Instead, the two former Island Tug & Barge hands attributed their courage to that casual disregard for danger held by most teenage boys. When Harold Elworthy congratulated them and then asked his new hands if they were now through with the seafaring life, they both replied, no, they were ready for their next voyage.

In this mid-1930s photo of the crew of the *Salvage Queen*, Joe Quilty is the boy to the right of the life ring and Captain Fred Cole—master of the *Anyox* at the time of the *Dunsyre* loss—is directly behind the life ring. JOE QUILTY COLLECTION

## Postscript

In January 1942, Island Tug & Barge lost another sailing ship barge conversion off the west coast of Vancouver Island—*Fibreboard*, which was originally the four-masted steel barque *Robert Duncan* built in Port Glasgow, Scotland, in 1891. Once again, all the bargees managed to get off safely. In my research into old sailing ships used for barge service in British Columbia, I've discovered that while a number of them succumbed to marine hazard, apparently no lives were ever lost.

"... not knowing where they were or when they would go ashore . . . their wind-driven ship passed through perilous waters; and after they had abandoned her in the lifeboat . . . they watched their late home destroyed in the surf right below Kains Island lighthouse." —November 21, 1936, Victoria *Times Colonist*. RICK JAMES COLLECTION

"For eighteen hours they were aboard the *Dunsyre*, with lifebelts strapped to them . . . They could hardly stand as the vessel was rolling and plunging so heavily. Yet throughout the night they kept their nerve . . ." —November 21, 1936, Victoria *Times Colonist*. RICK JAMES COLLECTION

# Chapter 16

# From Heroes to Hulks: The 1940s

A few months after the end of the Second World War, the War Assets Corporation, the government disposal agency, ran a nationwide advertisement announcing that "39 frigate-type ships declared surplus to Canadian Naval requirements . . ." were to be sold off "as is, where is." With the return of peace, Canada's federal government realized it could ill afford to maintain what had evolved during the war into one of the largest naval forces in the world, and put most of it on the block.

In the early years of the war Canada's fledgling navy, the Royal Canadian Navy (RCN) had found itself hard pressed to assist a beleaguered Great Britain. Lean Depression years' budgets had allowed for only a bare bones fleet of six destroyers, four minesweepers, a trawler and two small training vessels. In an attempt to curb the ever-increasing shipping losses to U-boats in the North Atlantic and the impending economic strangulation of Britain, Canadian industry undertook a massive shipbuilding program. Shipyards on both the west and east coasts, as well as in the Great Lakes, were soon actively immersed in building a substantial small-ship fighting force for the RCN.

With the return of peace, the federal government decided that the bulk of this wartime shipbuilding program (more than 350 fighting ships) was to be disposed of. Most, like the corvettes, were simply broken up if they weren't sold to a mercantile venture or to a Central or South American navy. Here on the West Coast, however, a number of the larger vessels—the minesweepers, corvettes and frigates—managed to find local peacetime employment.

The Union Steamship Company bought three Castle-class corvettes—HMCS *Leaside*, HMCS *St. Thomas* and HMCS *Hespeler*—for the bargain price of $75,000 each. After expensive conversions and the repainting of their drab wartime grey with bright white, the 1,060-ton-displacement, 252-foot corvettes were transformed into the SS *Coquitlam II*, SS *Camosun III* and SS *Chilcotin* and were soon recognized along the coast as the Union Steamship Company's White Boats.

Union Steamships also purchased four Bangor minesweepers—HMCS *Bellechasse*, *Miramichi*, *Courtenay* and *Chignecto*. The company hoped to convert and operate the 672-ton, 180-foot ships as a passenger express service but the plan was shelved. Although it was rumoured that a San Francisco firm had made an offer on them, no record apparently exists as to what actually became of the four minesweepers.

Victoria's Island Tug & Barge Company also bought one of the RCN veterans—the Flower-class corvette HMCS *Sudbury*. The towboat company equipped the 950-ton, 205-foot-long vessel for salvage work and the investment soon paid off; the corvettes were noted for their seakeeping abilities in the North Atlantic and *Sudbury* made an excellent deep-sea tug. The dramatic sea rescues performed by *Sudbury* soon

Lieutenant Commander R.W. "Bob" Draney, DSC RCNR ret., surveys his old wartime command, *K324*, at Royston. He happened to be mate on the tug *Florence Filberg* when they picked up the gutted hull of HMCS *Prince Rupert* to tow her to her final resting place. BOB DRANEY COLLECTION

earned Island Tug & Barge a high profile along the coast even though the company was primarily occupied with the more mundane job of towing logs, chips and hog fuel for their forest company clients.

When *Sudbury* arrived under Lions Gate Bridge in December 1955 with the Greek ship *Makedonia* under tow, thousands of local residents lined the shore cheering. The tug had just performed an incredible rescue. The freighter was picked up adrift with a damaged drive shaft off the Kamchatka peninsula and was then towed 3,500 miles through "gale lashed seas and stubborn currents," according to the *Vancouver Province*.

Along with a number of minesweepers and corvettes disposed of on the West Coast were 14 frigates. The frigate building program didn't start until well into the war and therefore the first of the "twin-screw corvettes," as the new design was originally called, didn't arrive for the Battle of the Atlantic until late in 1943. These efficient U-boat hunter-killers were soon discovered to be the ideal convoy escort vessel: they had twice the range of the smaller corvette and were better armed as well as being far more pleasant to be aboard. Around two-thirds of the 70 River-class frigates built for the RCN were paid off at the end of the war, even though most had experienced only a year, or two at most, of active war service since their launch.

Local Victoria scrap dealer Morris Greene of Capital Iron & Metals Ltd. was quick to notice the War Assets Corporation advertisement and he convinced his two partners, Izzy Stein and Harry

After 1945, the federal government disposed of all but a handful of the Royal Canadian Navy's wartime fleet. Here on the West Coast, the decommissioned vessels sat mothballed in Bedwell Bay, Indian Arm, waiting to be sold off by the War Assets Corporation. Circa 1946 photo. MARITIME MUSEUM OF BRITISH COLUMBIA P 3570 C

Wagner, that there was money to be made scrapping warships. Greene bought all 14 frigates that were put up for sale on the West Coast, as well as the Algerine-class minesweeper *Border Cities*. The firm of Wagner, Stein and Greene was established and a breaker's yard was set up at Ogden Point next to the grain elevator.

The first RCN ship to pass under the wrecker's torch, in January 1948, was *K324*, HMCS *Prince Rupert*, launched only five years earlier at the Yarrows Ltd. shipyard in Esquimalt. Once the ship had been stripped, the gutted hull was destined to be towed to Royston, BC, where she became part of a hulk breakwater to protect Comox Logging & Railway Company's log dump and booming ground. Through a strange quirk of fate, the tug sent to pick up the *K324* was *Florence Filberg*, which just happened to have on board as first mate retired Lieutenant Commander Robert Draney DSC, RCNR, from New Westminster. He had been the *Prince Rupert*'s commander during the Second World War.

After the *Prince Rupert* was dismantled and disposed of, efficiency rose to the point where the Ogden Point yard could completely scrap a ship in six weeks. Eleven more frigates were stripped and their hulls sold to logging companies who used them all for hulk breakwaters. HMCS *Dunver* and *Eastview* joined the *Prince Rupert* at Royston, while HMCS *Matane*, *Levis* and *Charlottetown* went to Iron River Logging's operation at Oyster Bay near Campbell River. Forest company giant Macmillan Bloedel purchased HMCS *Cape Breton*, *La Salle*, *Longueuil* and *Runnymede* for their Kelsey Bay Division and HMCS *Coaticook* for the floating hulk breakwater surrounding their big pulp and paper mill operation in Powell River. Two frigates that managed to escape the cutter's torch were HMCS *Kokanee* and HMCS *Waskesiu*, which were resold to the Indian government for conversion to Hooghly River pilot boats. (Two hulls that remain

HMCS *Sudbury*, which served in the Battle of the Atlantic, was one of over a hundred corvettes built for the Royal Canadian Navy during the Second World War. Unlike the frigates, nearly all the corvettes were disposed of at war's end. Most were scrapped but some were sold off, and the *Sudbury* ended up working as a towboat and salvage tug with Island Tug & Barge of Victoria. CFB ESQUIMALT NAVAL & MILITARY MUSEUM, NEG. F-3365

The dramatic sea rescues performed by the deep-sea salvage tug *Sudbury* soon earned Island Tug & Barge a high profile along the coast even though the company was primarily occupied with the more mundane job of towing logs, chips and hog fuel for their forest company clients. VANCOUVER MARITIME MUSEUM #12557

unaccounted for, and which were probably cut for scrap metal, are the frigate HMCS *Grou* and the minesweeper *Border Cities*.)

Wagner, Stein and Greene later scrapped the war-weary destroyer *H61*, HMCS *Gatineau*, which had already seen strenuous service as the Royal Navy's HMS *Express* before being turned over to the RCN early in 1943. The E-class destroyer was part of the Dunkirk rescue mission in the summer of 1940. *H61* made six trips to the besieged beach and after rescuing some 3,500 troops was reported to be the second-to-last ship to leave the area. While serving in the Far East as escort to the battle cruiser HMS *Repulse* and the battleship HMS *Prince of Wales* in December 1941, *Express* was on hand to take off nearly 1,000 officers and crew from the slowly capsizing *Prince of Wales* when both warships were sunk by Japanese planes off Malaya. Declared surplus in 1947, HMCS *Gatineau* was later broken up at Ogden Point and her stripped hull joined the three frigates at Royston.

Residents of Canada's East Coast are fortunate that they can visit two restored examples of the RCN's contribution to victory in the Battle of the Atlantic. The Flower-class corvette HMCS *Sackville* is open to the public in Halifax Harbour, while the Tribal-class destroyer HMCS *Haida* is berthed in Hamilton, Ontario. Here on the West Coast, even though a number of RCN warships that served in the Second World War were granted a reprieve and saw some active peacetime service, none remains afloat.

The destroyer *H61*, HMCS *Gatineau*, was scrapped at the Ogden Point ship-scrapping yard in Victoria's Outer Harbour in about 1948. The shipyard was organized by the firm of Wagner, Stein & Greene to deal with decommissioned RCN warships following the end of World War II. MARITIME MUSEUM OF BRITISH COLUMBIA P 4046 B

## Wagner, Stein and Greene

The Ogden Point ship-scrapping yard in Victoria's Outer Harbour was organized by the firm of Wagner, Stein & Greene primarily to deal with RCN warships bought from the War Assets Corporation. Morris Greene, originator of the project, owned the Capital Iron store on Store Street. Today, Capital Iron still serves as a popular hardware, clothing and recreational supplies outlet, as well as a surplus goods establishment, next to Victoria's Chinatown.

Greene got his start in the scrap business with a brother-in-law who owned Atlas Iron & Metals in Vancouver. They collected scrap, sorted it and sold the segregated material to dealers. In 1934 Greene went into partnership with Izzy Stein and Harry Wagner, forming Capital Iron & Metals Limited soon afterward. Wagner, Stein & Greene handled the Ogden Point ship-scrapping operation while Capital Iron & Metals Limited dealt with all non-ferrous metal.

In 1964, when it became too expensive to run two separate yards, the Ogden Point facility was closed. Ship dismantling at the dock behind Capital Iron continued to draw the nostalgic and the curious to the Store Street business until the early 1970s. While rusted hulls no longer clutter the dock, photographs of the scrapped ships adorn walls and pillars throughout the store, and bits of salvaged wood and brass ship paraphernalia still attract customers to the surplus department in the basement.

## Chapter 17

# Royston's Ship Graveyard, 1940s–1960s

Scattered just off the beach along the inside waters of British Columbia's southern coast are several collections of badly deteriorated and rusted remains of ships' hulls. While forest companies normally chose protected bays, coves and inlets to dump their logs and sort them into booms, on occasion they had to operate in areas exposed to strong tides, currents and foul weather. As a result, timber companies working out of Kelsey Bay near Sayward, Royston near Courtenay and Oyster River near Campbell River,

The bow of the three-masted ship *Riversdale* still stands proud off the beach of the small east Vancouver Island community of Royston. The bow of what was once the massive four-masted barque *Comet*, standing to seaward in the fog, has long since fallen over. RICK JAMES PHOTO, 1982

along with the pulp and paper mill at Powell River, have used the stripped hulls of retired ships to build protective breakwaters.

At Royston, directly across the bay from the town of Comox, there is one of the largest and most unusual of these hulk collections. It consists of the remains of four Royal Canadian Navy warships, one United States Navy destroyer, two whalers, two Canadian Pacific Railway steam tugs, a deep-sea rescue tug and, from the vanished days of commercial sailing, a wood-hulled barquentine and an auxiliary schooner, along with three massive Cape Horn windjammers.

The first hulk to arrive and be sunk at the site was the five-masted lumber schooner *Laurel Whalen* (see Chapter 9) in 1936. Once Comox Logging & Railway Company realized how effective the old lumber freighter's hull was in protecting their log dump, they began accumulating more retired vessels to scuttle on the weather side of their booming grounds. Together, in their varying states of deterioration, the grounded fleet of 14 vessels soon came to represent a fascinating cross-section of West Coast maritime history.

After *Laurel Whalen* was beached in 1936, it was to be another 10 years before more hulks arrived at Royston. On April 12, 1946, referring to the Canadian Pacific Railway Company's collier, the *Vancouver News Herald* announced, "Old *Melanope* to End Days as a Breakwater" (see Chapter 6.) Once they, too, were deemed no longer essential to the CPR's requirements, two steam-powered workhorses, the 305-gross-ton,

Some 135 years after her launching in Liverpool in 1876, the proud bow of the *Melanope* still remains upright at Royston. Just in front of her, the rusted remains of a triple expansion engine and boiler mark the last of the steam tug *Qualicum*. The *Melanope* may well have ended up on the towline behind the *Qualicum* at one time or another while serving as a collier in the CPR fleet. RICK JAMES PHOTO

116-foot-long tug *Nanoose* and the 200-ton, 96-foot *Qualicum*, were also turned over to Comox Logging & Railway. Part of either tug's working routine may have included towing the blackened collier *Melanope* from Ladysmith or Union Bay, the West Coast's principal coaling stations, to Burrard Inlet, where she would often be seen loading the bunkers of a graceful trans-Pacific Empress liner.

Courtenay resident Rolf Bruhn figures it was early in 1947 when the gutted hull of the American destroyer *Tattnall* was towed up from Puget Sound to Royston. At the time, Bruhn was a deckhand on the tug that undertook the job, the *Florence Filberg*, owned by Canadian Tug Boat, a sister company to Comox Logging & Railway.

The *Tattnall* is one of the many fleet destroyers mass produced in the United States during and just after the First World War. Commissioned on June 26, 1919, the 1,090-ton, 314-foot-long Wickes-class flush-decker (Canadian sailors called them four-stackers) did see some serious action in the Second World War. In July 1943 the *Tattnall* was transformed into *APD-19* after conversion into a high-speed "Destroyer Personnel Transport." She took part in a number of actions in the Mediterranean, including the disembarking of "Frederick's Freighters," the handpicked Americans and Canadians of the 1st Special Service Force, the "Devil's Brigade," at the heavily fortified Hyeres Islands, east of Toulon, France. Reassigned to the Pacific War in the spring of 1945, she joined the picket line of ships protecting the invasion fleet's anchorage off Okinawa in April 1945. *APD-19, Tattnall,* won three battle stars for her Second World War service.

Off the end of the breakwater, by the disjointed and broken sections of the three CPR vessels, lie the remnants of one, if not two, Consolidated Whaling Company whalers—the 102-ton, 92-foot-long *Blue* and *Black*. It is estimated that some 25,000 whales were taken by vessels like these throughout the 52 years that the shore-based whaling industry operated in British Columbia. From 1911 until their final disposal in 1947, these small ships were often seen during their winter lay-up at the Consolidated Whaling docks beside the Point Ellice Bridge in Victoria. Very little remains to identify them as whalers today—only a jagged hole in a foredeck of one entirely collapsed hull where a harpoon gun was removed many years ago by a local diver.

The largest component of scrapped hulls lying at Royston consists of four Royal Canadian Navy (RCN) ships that all arrived at the site in the post-war years of 1947 and 1948. The history of these ships—the frigates HMCS *Prince Rupert*, *Eastview* and *Dunver,* and the 1,370-ton, 326-foot-long E-class destroyer HMCS *Gatineau*—is discussed in detail in the previous chapter.

Another scrapped hull at Royston that saw service in the Second World War was the US Navy fleet rescue tug *ATR 13*. This "auxiliary tug rescue" was one of nearly 100 ocean-going fleet rescue tugs built in the United States during the war. These 164-foot salvage vessels were originally designed for firefighting and for towing damaged ships from the scene of battle.

Seventeen-year-old Leo Murphy, looking to his first draft and fresh out of navy diesel school, boarded the brand new *ATR 13* in December 1943 only to discover she had a steam power plant, not a diesel. He caught on quickly, nonetheless, and *ATR 13* crossed the Atlantic the following March to join a fleet of tugs with tandem tows of barges all required for the invasion of Fortress Europe.

Murphy and the rescue tug saw their first action off the D-Day beaches in the summer of 1944. In September that same year, already a seasoned veteran of Sicily, Salerno and Anzio, as well as Normandy, *ATR 13* was sent to the war in the Pacific where she became one of the first Allied ships to enter the Sasebo naval base on the island of Kyushu following the Japanese surrender in August 1945.

Deemed no longer "essential to the defence of US," the tug was sold to the Pacific Salvage Company of Vancouver, BC, in late August 1947. The company quickly renamed their new acquisition *Salvage King* and fitted her out with the latest in electronic equipment and 350 fathoms of two-inch steel cable. Since the deep-sea tug also had a towing radius of 7,000 miles, her new owners proudly claimed she was "the best equipped salvage ship afloat." Unfortunately, her firefighting equipment—consisting of two pumps and five monitors capable of discharging 3,000 gallons of water per minute—proved useless when she herself caught fire in Victoria Harbour in October 1953. Found too damaged to repair, the charred ruin was stripped by Capital Iron and eventually towed to Royston in 1959. The wooden hull of *Salvage King,* ex-*ATR 13,* finally succumbed to the elements some years ago and there's little left to identify her anymore.

In the centre of the breakwater, surrounded by rock ballast, lies a massive wooden hull with large timbered ribs, the last remains of the five-masted barquentine *Forest Friend* (whom we met in Chapter 14), which arrived at Royston sometime in the late 1950s. Built in Aberdeen, Washington, in 1919, the 1,614-gross-ton, 243-foot *Forest Friend* was one of a large fleet of wood schooner-style vessels constructed along the Pacific Northwest during the First World War. For some 75 years, US sawmill owners built up a sizeable fleet of lumber schooners and barquentines for both the coastwise and trans-Pacific trades. As a result, the lumber industry in the US northwest was able to rely on a fleet of some 300 sailing vessels registered to both lumber mill companies and independent ship owners to freight their product to local and overseas markets.

In 1922, a 17-year-old Bent Sivertz signed up on the five-masted barquentine *Forest Friend* while she was loading lumber at Hastings Mill. He recalled that the *Forest Friend* was "wartime construction—no frills," but nonetheless "she was fortunate in having an excellent naval architect and first class shipwrights." In this photo the towline has just been dropped and all sails are nearly set as she passes out of Juan de Fuca Strait headed across the Pacific with a load of lumber. SAN FRANCISCO MARITIME NHP, J.8,990N

*Forest Friend* (on the right in this photo) probably arrived at Comox Logging & Railway Company's hulk break-water sometime in the mid-1950s. The last remains of the Cape Horn windjammer *Riversdale* stand beside her, scuttled at the site in November 1961. COURTESY COURTENAY, BC, NATIVE SONS HALL

In late September 1922, a young Bent Sivertz happened to see *Forest Friend* berthed alongside the Hastings Mill dock in Vancouver preparing to load a cargo of lumber for Sydney, Australia. Sivertz was able to secure a berth on the ship as an ordinary sailor after skilful exaggeration of his knowledge on the points of the compass and of knotting and splicing. Once she had set sail, the teenager was soon going through the purgatory of "learning the ropes" that every new sailor faced on a sailing ship.

*Forest Friend* remained in the offshore lumber trade for four more years and was then laid up idle on the Fraser River for a number of years before being sold to the Island Tug & Barge Company in 1937. The retired lumber freighter was subsequently cut down by the big forest product towing company and converted into a wood chip and hog fuel barge. Once she had reached the end of her working life, sometime in the 1950s, she was picked up by Comox Logging and shoved in next to the A-frame at the new truck log dump that had just been built at Royston.

The most prominent remaining feature of the Royston hulk collection, standing just off the beach, is the proud Victorian bow of the steel, three-masted Cape Horn windjammer *Riversdale*. Launched from Liverpool, England, in 1894, the 2,206-ton, 276-foot *Riversdale* was a prime example of a British-built square-rigger of the late nineteenth century. In the days before steamships came to dominate the sea lanes of the world, thousands of windjammers such as *Riversdale* were running before the trade winds in the deepwater trade.

*Riversdale* was in and out of ports around the world over the next 20 years, wherever sailing ships were required to transport the bulk cargoes then in high demand, such as coal, coke, lumber and wheat. While carrying coke to the Gulf of Mexico in the summer of 1914, as the German-owned *Harvestehude*, the ship found herself in the smelter port of Santa Rosalia when war broke out in Europe. Along with 11 other German square-riggers, the Cape Horn windjammer remained interned in the hot and desolate harbour, her decks drying in the Mexican sun and barnacles collecting on her anchor chains, for the duration of the war.

In 1924, after the Santa Rosalia collection of German windjammers were awarded to the victors of the Great War, *Riversdale* was bought by American lumberman Robert Dollar, but she was laid up in San Francisco and never sailed again. In 1924, the deteriorating ship was bought by the Coastwise Steamship & Barge Company of Vancouver, who cut her down into a barge and used her for hauling ore from the Anyox mine in northern BC to a Tacoma, Washington, smelter. Then, in 1935, she joined a fleet of 12 other retired sailing ships owned by Island Tug & Barge Company, all purchased as cheap bottoms to haul chips, hog fuel and logs along the coast.

By the late 1950s, *Riversdale* had passed into the hands of the Crown Zellerbach Corporation, who renamed the log barge *Crown Zellerbach #3*. When her hull started to show its age and began to give out after withstanding years of being smashed and beaten by logs dropped into her holds, Crown Zellerbach towed her into Comox Harbour to be scuttled on the outside of Royston's hulk breakwater (the big

Eric Lawson, who had an extensive career specializing in wood conservation in the field of historic ship preservation, inspects a scupper door along the port side of the barquentine *Forest Friend* at Royston in 1994. RICK JAMES PHOTO

American forest company Crown Zellerbach now owned the site, having bought Comox Logging & Railway Company in the early 1950s).

Just to the seaward of *Crown Zellerbach #3* (ex-*Riversdale)* lie the remains of another massive log barge, *Crown Zellerbach #2.* This hulk was originally launched as the four-masted barque *Comet* from a shipyard in Port Glasgow, Scotland, in 1901. The massive steel square-rigger was purpose-built to carry "case-oil" kerosene. By the late 1880s the worldwide demand for case-oil was growing at a phenomenal rate and ever-increasing quantities were being shipped from Standard Oil refineries along the US eastern seaboard. Eight large sailing ships specially designed as case-oil carriers were some of the largest square-riggers ever to be launched from British shipyards. The four-masted steel barque *Comet* measured some 318 feet in length and was registered as 3,017 gross tons. Later, while in the hands of a German shipping company as *Orotava*, the big Cape Horn windjammer also found herself interned in the Mexican port of Santa Rosalia for the duration of the Great War.

Lumberman Robert Dollar, who bought all 12 square-riggers interned in Mexico and brought them up to San Francisco, had *Orotava* (ex-*Comet*) make one lumber voyage across the Pacific, but commercial sailing was no longer viable and the barque was sold off to Pacific (Coyle) Navigation Company of Vancouver in 1929. She was promptly cut down into the barge *Pacific Forester* and remained with Pacific (Coyle) until sold to Island Tug & Barge in 1936 to become *Island Forester.*

After the Second World War, Island Tug mounted three large steam cranes on the *Island Forester*'s deck for loading and unloading logs. Like *Riversdale*, *Island Forester* was finally sold to Crown Zellerbach who renamed her *Crown Zellerbach #2*, and in 1962 the old windjammer joined her sister barge at Royston.

The weather and sea have taken a harsh toll on the breakwater's fleet of hulks, and every passing year weakens the structural integrity of yet another hulk to the point at which it collapses into more broken and rusted rubble. Field Sawmill has vacated the mill site on the Courtenay River, so the breakwater no longer fulfils any useful purpose anyway. All the same, the ships served useful roles far beyond their original builders' expectations, and with their varied histories reaching well back into the nineteenth century they have not only provided more than 50 years of service as a hulk breakwater but also constitute an important maritime heritage site.

# Chapter 18

# The *Brig. Gen. M.G. Zalinski*: 60 Years Lost in Grenville Channel, 1946

Archie McLaren couldn't sleep one particularly stormy night in September 1946—he was quite disturbed about the weather conditions as his ship, *Brig. Gen. M.G. Zalinski*, ran full speed ahead up Grenville Channel in BC's Inside Passage. As the Transportation Agent (purser) aboard the steamer, McLaren was so convinced that they were headed for a disaster that he woke up the ship's clerk to help him prepare to abandon ship if need be. The two wrapped up the ship's records in heavy paper and ensured that all the cash aboard was in the money bag and ready to grab at a moment's notice. McLaren also had the foresight to slip some other valuables into the bag—two bottles of bourbon. His disturbing premonition held true. Disaster struck *Brig. Gen. M.G. Zalinski* within a couple of hours.

Around 3:00 a.m. on September 29, the crew of *Brig. Gen. M.G. Zalinski* were shaken from their sleep when the ship suddenly received a severe jolt that was quickly followed by emergency blasts of the ship's whistle. *Zalinski* was already listing to starboard and taking on water quickly by the time the crew lined up to get in the lifeboats. The US Army Transport ship had struck rocks off Pitt Island, a few miles from Lowe Inlet.

The cargo ship *Brig. Gen. M.G. Zalinski* was originally launched in 1919 as the steel freighter *Lake Frohna*, hull #759 of the American Ship Building Co., Lorain, Ohio, for the United States Shipping Board (USSB). Built as a Laker-class ship, she was a full canal-sized ocean freighter of the common three-island, four-hatch, two-masted type. The canal-sized ships were limited to some 260 feet in length in order to access the Atlantic ocean via the American and Canadian canal and inland waterway systems.

Severe shortages of ocean-going ships brought on by the onset of the First World War had resulted in the creation of the USSB in September 1916. When the US entered the war in April 1917, a subsidiary of the Shipping Board, the Emergency Fleet Corporation, was assigned government authority to acquire, construct and operate merchant vessels. Its job was to build a "bridge of ships" across the Atlantic Ocean to deliver munitions and supplies to the US troops in Europe.

By the time *Lake Frohna* was completed in 1919, however, the Great War was over (the Armistice was signed on November 11, 1918). Apparently the USSB had the Laker on a trans-Atlantic run for a short time but then, in 1924, *Lake Frohna* and three other surplus cargo ships were purchased from the USSB by Alexander McDougall of the Minnesota Atlantic Transit Co. in Duluth, Minnesota. *Lake Frohna* was renamed *Ace* while the other three were renamed *King*, *Queen* and *Jack*, and the four ships became known as the "Poker Fleet." They were operated between the Lakehead at Duluth and Buffalo, Ohio, on Lake Erie

*Brig. Gen. M.G. Zalinski* is shown here as a US Army Transport Service vessel, probably at Seattle's Port of Embarkation during the war. According to crewman Archie McLaren, the former Great Lakes freighter, formerly *Ace*, was well suited to her role hauling supplies to Alaska, being highly manoeuvrable. PUGET SOUND MARITIME HISTORICAL SOCIETY 1050-1

carrying package freight—any freight that was sacked, bagged, bundled or cased—as well as other general merchandise and assembled goods. However, the Poker Fleet became best known for hauling automobiles by the thousands throughout the 1920s, and the freighters were often seen departing Detroit, Michigan, with deckloads of shiny new Ford Model Ts. The package freight industry itself went into a slow decline and finally disappeared during the Second World War when traffic on the Great Lakes began to carry bulk materials.

With the US about to enter WW II late in 1941, *Ace* was purchased by the US Army in September of that year and, after requisitioning by the Quartermaster Corps, the ship was renamed US Army Transport (USAT) *Brigadier General M.G. Zalinski* and transferred to Seattle. The old Laker was used throughout the war primarily for transporting supplies to Alaska. *Zalinski* remained on this Alaska run right up until the night it was lost.

The Puget Sound Pilots' movement cards revealed that *Brig. Gen. M.G. Zalinski* was assigned late in September 1946 to carry perishables to Alaska because a strike was tying up Puget Sound ports at the time. The ship was destined for Whittier with 1,115 tons of meat, fresh fruit and vegetables in its refrigerated holds and 778 tons of general cargo aboard, including household goods for military personnel.

In the March 1988 issue of *Sea Chest: The Journal of the Puget Sound Maritime Historical Society*, Archie K. McLaren, an officer on *Brig. Gen. M.G. Zalinski*, related his first-hand account of the ship's loss. He began by pointing out that *Zalinski*, as a former Laker, ". . . was considered very adaptable to the Alaskan trade as it was only 260 feet long and easy to maneuver in restricted areas."

McLaren recalled that on previous voyages *Zalinski* had usually called at Seward in order to discharge cargo to railcars destined for Anchorage, but that on the final voyage the ship was bound for Whittier, closer to Anchorage. The ship left Seattle in the early morning of September 26, and McLaren described the rain that night as ". . . so heavy that one could not distinguish rain drops falling. It was more like a wall . . ." To make matters worse, only one of the ship's two pilots had boarded in Seattle, a Captain Thorvick who ". . . was well past 70 years of age . . ." and who, the crew soon realized, was also past his professional prime. As McLaren described it, from the moment of departure from Seattle, the voyage seemed to be jinxed and ". . . there was only one kind of weather . . . BAD!"

*Brig. Gen. M.G. Zalinski* was not equipped with radar and was attempting to navigate the Inside Passage the old-fashioned way—by bouncing the ship's whistle-blasts off the shore and measuring the elapsed time for the returning echo to determine distance from land. "To this day, I can recall the gaunt

The *Lake Frohna* became the *Ace* as part of the Minnesota-Atlantic Transit Company's "Poker Fleet." The *Ace*, *King*, *Queen* and *Jack*—while primarily occupied transporting packaged freight around the Great Lakes—were best known for hauling automobiles out of Detroit. LAKE SUPERIOR MARITIME COLLECTIONS, UNIVERSITY OF WISCONSIN-SUPERIOR
MCK #15389

face of Captain Thorvick after two days or more standing watch . . . around the clock," McLaren remembered in his account.

The ship dropped anchor for a brief respite but Captain Joseph N. Zardis, impatient to be underway again before daylight, sent for Thorvick after only four or five hours of rest. The elderly pilot protested, noting that they were very close to Grenville Channel where it would be next to impossible to navigate with the heavy rain muffling all sound, but the captain ignored him. As he listened to the rumble of the anchor windlass Archie McLaren was certain that the ship wasn't going to get through the night without eventually hitting one side of the channel or the other.

On Monday, September 30, the *Prince Rupert Daily News* reported that *Brig. Gen. M.G. Zalinski* had ". . . gone aground and sunk by the bow within minutes early Sunday morning. Running (full speed) parallel to the shore, she grounded on rocks, crumpling her steel plates amidships like paper and opening a hole through which the water poured rapidly. The veteran transport sank 25 minutes later . . . without even the final salute of exploding boilers."

All 48 of *Zalinski's* crew and a red setter, which was being shipped to Lieut. Col. G.E. Dawson of Anchorage, were able to get away in the two port-side lifeboats. Drifting in the channel, they watched their ship slowly settle into the sea. Two or three hours later they were picked up by the fish packer *Sally N* and were taken to the Canadian Fishing Company's cannery at Butedale, and then to Prince Rupert aboard the Union Steamship's *Catala*.

In Prince Rupert, winch operator Bernard Boersema told a reporter, "Driving rain made it so black we couldn't even see the bow when we struck. The force of the collision broke No. 1 and No. 2 holds clear open—a tear about 40 feet long. When the mate asked me to sound the bilge in the two holds there were already seven feet of water in No. 1 and more rushing in like fury." Boersema was told to forget about sounding No. 2 hold and to head for a lifeboat.

With Captain Zardis apparently in a state of shock it fell upon Archie McLaren to contact the Seattle Port of Embarkation by radiophone and make a report. When asked whether it was possible to salvage the ship, McLaren replied, "Sure, if you know of a company that could pull it off in some 400 to 500 feet of water."

*Brig. Gen. M.G. Zalinski* remained forgotten on the sea bottom off Pitt Island for 60 years. Then, on May 11, 2006, the ship was back in the news once again. The *Vancouver Sun* reported that, "The Canadian government—fearing a 700-tonne oil spill and even a massive underwater explosion—is seeking international help to deal with a bomb-laden, oil-leaking American army transport vessel . . ." Apparently Canadian Coast Guard officials were alerted in 2003 when an extensive oily sheen was spotted on the surface of Grenville Channel near the wreck site. Twice divers were sent down to seal the leaks but no further work was carried out because of concern about the unexploded ordinance believed to include a dozen approximately 500-pound aerial bombs, as well as .30 and .50 calibre ammunition.

While the depth in Grenville Channel is approximately 300 feet, the wreck came to rest on a ledge only about 100 feet below the surface, depending on the tide height. A warning was issued in January 2004 ordering mariners to avoid anchoring or fishing within 650 feet of the wreck. One of the fears was that the ship was well within reach of recreational divers. There was also concern expressed for the numerous cruise ships that pass through Grenville Channel, sometimes only about 300 feet from the hazardous wreck's location.

# Chapter 19

# A Stranding on Porter Reef:
# The Loss of the *North Sea*, 1947

As *North Sea*, an American cargo and passenger steamer, made its way south across Milbanke Sound in the early evening of February 13, 1947, it was raining so hard that the lights at both Susan and Vancouver Rocks were obscured. A 30-knot southeaster was blowing on the starboard beam and the seas were choppy. As she turned into Seaforth Channel, the Ivory Island and then Idol Point lights were momentarily visible but then vanished from sight in the rainy haze.

Finally, at 21:43 hours and travelling at full speed under the command of Captain Charles C. Graham, *North Sea* slammed into Porter Reef on the north shore of Seaforth Channel and came to a stop with a

The passenger and freight steamer *North Sea* was on a regular run from Puget Sound to Alaska in the late 1930s, with voyages usually terminating at the historic city of Sitka. To the great interest of the tourists aboard, the *North Sea* also stopped at cannery ports during the summer salmon season. On one trip the ship returned to Seattle with 56,000 cases aboard, along with her full passenger list. VANCOUVER MARITIME MUSEUM PR 3476

crashing jolt. Bilges were sounded immediately and, when it was discovered that #1 starboard was taking on water fast and #2 hold, which contained ice boxes, was flooded up to the 'tween decks with water still pouring in, an SOS was immediately transmitted. As well as 60 crew and 85 passengers, there were some 167 tons of frozen fish, 50 tons of general cargo and 70 tons of baggage aboard.

*North Sea* had departed Seattle on January 29, 1947, with a full load of cargo and passengers aboard. A northerly gale with blizzard conditions had buffeted the ship as it progressed north up Lynn Canal, and it was necessary to break ice through the narrow channels leading to Sitka. On the return trip south the weather finally warmed up but it began to rain hard once *North Sea* left Ketchikan, and the rain persisted all the way to Milbanke Sound and into Seaforth Channel where *North Sea* ran up onto Porter Reef.

At the time of the stranding the 1,903-ton, 299-foot *North Sea* was nearly 30 years old. She was originally launched in 1918 as the standard three-island type steel freighter *Plainfield* by S. Moore & Sons Shipbuilding Co. in Elizabethport, New Jersey. During the First World War the ship was under the control of the United States Shipping Board, but whether *Plainfield* went into lay-up after the war with hundreds of other American freighters is unknown at the time of writing. It is known that the vessel entered commercial service when the Baltimore and Carolina Steamship Co. purchased two Shipping Board vessels, *Tipton* and *Plainfield*, in 1922, renamed them *Esther Weems* and *Mary Weems* respectively and converted them into passenger vessels for service on a Baltimore–Charleston–Miami run.

Around 1927 both ships were sold to the Pacific Steamship Company of Seattle. *Esther Weems* became *Admiral Benson* and *Mary Weems* was named *Admiral Peoples*. The latter ship was soon recognized as one of the line's finest, with her private bathrooms, shower and toilet facilities. Clinton H. Betz, in his history of the Pacific Steamship Company in the September 1990 issue of *Sea Chest: The Journal of the Puget Sound Maritime Historical Society*, commented, "The ships were far from being graceful or good-looking vessels, possessing no rake or sheer and with straight up-and-down masts and funnels. Clearly noticeable was their origin as freighters. They were rated as 'fair' passenger ships."

By early 1930 *Admiral Peoples* was on a California–Puget Sound route and in 1934 she was sold to the Northland Transportation Company of Seattle and refurbished to carry 500 tons of cold storage cargo. Renamed *North Sea*, the passenger and freight liner was placed on the Puget Sound to Southeast Alaska run. For the duration of the Second World War the Northland Transportation fleet was under the control of the War Services Administration, but with the return of peace in 1945 the ships were released back to Northland. With her machinery overhauled and accommodations refurbished to passenger-liner standards, *North Sea* was returned to the Alaska run.

As it happened, on the night of her mishap BC Packers' herring fleet was tied up at Bella Bella waiting out the foul weather and, upon hearing *North Sea*'s distress signal, some of the larger boats (*North Isle, Bernice L, Cape Henry, Three Aces, Nishga* and *Otter Bay*) raced to the scene. Between 0015 and 0100 hours a rescue fleet composed of fish boats, tugboats and a Fisheries patrol boat evacuated all 85 passengers and most of the crew and returned them to Bella Bella. (The corpse that was being shipped south and reposed in the baggage locker wasn't to be "rescued" until two days later.) A day later, the southbound Canadian National steamer *Prince Rupert* stopped at Bella Bella, picked up the passengers and crew and took them to Vancouver. The *Prince Rupert* reported that she had just gone through "the worst storm in her history."

Meanwhile the stricken *North Sea* was starting to pound while water rapidly filled her engine room and holds. As the tug *La Garde* stood by, the tug *La Pointe* held a line secure on *North Sea*'s bow while anchors were put out in case the ship showed signs of shifting on the reef. The pumps on board were activated and additional pumps arrived with the Pacific Salvage Company's *Salvage Chieftain* on February 16. Efforts to

Loaded with tons of fish that soon began to decompose, the stranded *North Sea* became home to hordes of rats that descended into the holds to eat their fill each time the tide receded, as Syd Woodside, the customs superintendent in Prince Rupert, was to discover. VANCOUVER MARITIME MUSEUM

wrest the *North Sea* free on the high tides proved futile. Also, as recorded in Chief Officer Frank Huxtable's report: ". . . Strict Watch was kept to protect ship's property from salvage crew . . ."

He noted further on February 28, ". . . Rechecked all rooms and crew's quarters and found several doors unlocked and rooms broken into . . . 4:00 p.m. found Chief Engineer's room broken into and several items missing. Reported to salvage boss and Canadian Customs."

On March 5, tugs *Salvage Chieftain* and *J.R. Morgan* made fast to *North Sea*'s stern and made several attempts to pull the ship off Porter Reef. On the third try *North Sea* began to pound heavily in the seas, and finally rolled 40 degrees to port, which dislodged the foremast. Then, at 1600 hours, loud cracking noises were heard. At this point all pumping was stopped as it was feared *North Sea* was about to break in two. Two hours later the salvage superintendent reported that the fire-room bulkhead had been carried away and a 40-foot crack had appeared along the port side. At this point, he declared the vessel a total constructive loss. On March 7, the ship's owner ordered the ship abandoned.

The Coast Guard investigation concluded on March 20, and Captain George Hansen, the pilot, was cleared of the charge of "inattention to duty." *North Sea* was insured for $500,000 at the time of loss. Stores and other items aboard the derelict steamship were soon looted, while the hull itself was sold to BC interests who stripped the wreck of its winches, all moveable machinery, lifeboats etc., as well as anything of value from the passenger accommodations. What remained of the steamship was sold to an Oceans Falls agent for a Victoria scrap firm.

Later in the summer of 1947 Syd Woodside, customs superintendent in Prince Rupert, went on board *North Sea* and discovered swarms of rats as the sole occupants. Apparently, they were descending into the holds at low tide to take their fill of the 15 car loads of rotten fish and then making their way topsides again on the incoming tide. "I had thousands of them watching the last time I was on board," Woodside said. "It was an eerie experience."

Campbell River resident Bob Logan, who happened to live at Shearwater from 1947 to 1950, thinks the Ocean Falls agent who acquired the salvage rights to *North Sea* was named Harold Hunter. He was also told that it was Andy Carrie of Oceans Falls who took Hunter out to *North Sea* with his tug *Bonnie Belle* to take a look at the propeller. Carrie thought he could position a barge directly behind *North Sea* and, once they had removed the propeller nut and rudder, blow the propeller directly off onto the barge. Logan figured they were successful since Carrie returned from the adventure with the propeller on board the barge.

Once Hunter had finished salvaging what he wanted, he turned over the rights to Andy Widsten of Widsten and Logan Marine. They went alongside the derelict with a 56-foot landing barge and some salvage gear two or three times over the next couple of years and managed to retrieve lengths of cable and deck-benches, which they used around Shearwater until they finally rotted out. They also recovered the ship's gangplank, which was used for many years as a Shearwater wharf ramp. In his Letter to the Editor in the July 2009 *Western Mariner,* Logan noted that when they were aboard *North Sea* salvaging what they could, they never saw any rats.

*North Sea* stood out on Porter Reef as a sentinel to passing ships for years afterward. When passing the wreck at night the CPR coast steamers would floodlight the remains of the forlorn steamer for the benefit of their passengers but, by 1963, time, tide and weather had taken their toll and *North Sea* collapsed and disappeared beneath the waves.

UASBC diver Sheldon Boyd explores the wreck of the *North Sea* in the waters close to Porter Reef. JACQUES MARC PHOTO

*Chapter 20*

# Coastal Treasures: Fred Rogers, BC's "Wreck Diver Emeritus," 2008

When Fred Rogers slipped into the turbulent waters of Porlier Pass, the narrow tidal passage between Valdez and Galiano Islands in BC's Georgia Strait, he was in for a shock. "The force of the tide was alarming, holding us out on a horizontal plane like a flag on a pole," he describes in his book *Shipwrecks of British Columbia*. Even worse than that, Fred recalled, ". . . any attempt at turning our head sideways to the current was trouble; it would tear away your face-mask or mouth-piece."

It was Easter 1955 and Rogers was making his very first wreck dive with buddy Pat Moloney. Their target was the steam tug *Point Grey*, which had struck a reef and sunk in Porlier Pass in February 1949. The wreck, shuddering in the tide and appearing as if it might topple off the reef at any time, held Rogers in awe of its violent beauty. Even now, more than 50 years later, he still defines his *Point Grey* experience as, "The one that opened my eyes; we were now addicts for more adventure."

The hunt for shipwrecks became an obsession that was to take Rogers along most of BC's heavily convoluted coastline. When asked how many wrecks he actually dove on over his career, he simply points to the bookshelves loaded with his logbooks and glibly says, "It's all up there if you want to count 'em!" Still, even without an accurate tally of his efforts, Rogers was always aware of the significance of what he was doing and kept meticulous records. When he hung up his tank and flippers for good, he sat down and published all his West Coast diving endeavours in three books.

Fred Rogers' lifelong curiosity about the mysterious world beneath the ocean's surface started at an early age. When he was growing up in the Grandview district of Vancouver in the 1930s he would often take the streetcar down to Stanley Park to fish for bullheads. There Fred observed his first real divers. They were laying a high-pressure water line across First Narrows. As he watched, fascinated with the hard-hat divers, it occurred to young Fred that there was far more on this earth than just the terrestrial world he inhabited.

The 15-year-old caused quite a sensation when he arrived at Stanley Park with his own homemade diving helmet. He had scrutinized photos of the internationally renowned diver William Beebe and realized that his dive helmet looked quite similar to the top of a galvanized hot water tank, so the teenager cut the top off a discarded water tank to fashion his own helmet. To make it more comfortable he wrapped a section of garden hose around the edge as a seal and had his dad cut a square for a viewing glass. Then Fred proceeded to wade into Burrard Inlet up to his neck. But he slipped on a rock, fell over, and his home-built hard hat instantly flooded with water. Diving was suddenly a less appealing pursuit. Fred decided to postpone his sub-sea experiments until some future time.

Fred Rogers purchased his first dry suit, mask and snorkel in the mid-1950s and saved money by making his own compressed air tank from a fire extinguisher. Diving soon became an important part of his life. FRED ROGERS COLLECTION

It was well into the 1950s when Rogers, again eager to see beneath the sea, purchased his first dry suit, fins, mask and snorkel in Seattle. It was an early Bell Aqua dry suit made of a very thin rubber that was easily punctured by barnacles. To save a few bucks he made his own weight belt and compressed air tank. The belt was straightforward, but the tank? His solution was a $5 fire extinguisher from the local junkyard. Once he had the gear and had taught himself how to dive, Rogers started picking up small jobs, such as clearing cable or rope caught in the props of towboats to supplement the family income. Following a wartime stint in the Royal Canadian Navy, he had found full-time work as a welder and pipefitter, so diving was still primarily a hobby that he had to schedule time for on weekends and holidays.

Then Pat Moloney got Rogers interested in hunting for shipwrecks. Moloney had begun compiling an inventory of wrecks from the Vancouver Pilotage office and Fred was amazed at the staggering number of vessels that had been lost along the BC coastline over the previous century. The wreck diving would obviously require a very systematic approach. The two divers began by exploring the waters around Vancouver. Off Prospect Point in Stanley Park (where the teenaged Rogers had donned his first homemade diving gear) Rogers and three other divers were the first, in September 1960, to see the remains of one of the most famous ships on Canada's West Coast, the Hudson's Bay Company's SS *Beaver*. She had grounded there in 1888 and, four years later, the wake from the side-wheeler *Yosemite* had swept her off the rocks into deep water.

When they finished exploring local Lower Mainland waters and were ready to work further afield, Rogers and his diving partner Ed Seaton built themselves a 35-foot steel boat to take them upcoast in the winter of 1961–62. The following summer, their first major excursion would be to the wreck of *Themis* near Scarlett Point lighthouse off the northern end of Vancouver Island.

Aware that they were probably the first ever to see the wreck, the two divers were dazzled by what they found. "It was a mass of colour with its profusion of sea life," recalled Fred. "Then, as we moved along the side, a towering shadow confronted us through the disintegrated hull plating—the huge triple expansion steam engine, leaning as if about to fall over." While finding and exploring shipwrecks certainly had its romantic appeal and adventure, Rogers soon learned that it also had extreme hazards.

In the summer of 1964 Rogers, with his son Glenn and Ed Seaton, took their dive boat about 350 miles up the Inside Passage past Bella Bella to where the former freight and passenger steamship *Ohio* had

When they had finished exploring local Lower Mainland waters and were ready to work further afield, Fred Rogers and his diving partner, Eddie Seaton, built themselves this 35-foot steel boat in the winter of 1961–62 to take them upcoast. Here, Seaton is pictured alongside the wreck of the *Drumrock* in Takush Harbour. FRED ROGERS COLLECTION

been run ashore in Carter Bay in August 1909 after hitting a rock at Steep Point in Heikish Narrows. For a week the wreck divers gradually worked their way into the dark bowels of the *Ohio*, overwhelmed by all they found. One of the most unusual and puzzling relics was a large white bathtub containing hundreds of bottles with some of the necks protruding out of the black muck that permeated the wreck. Some of the bottles were still sealed with their corks and later Rogers and Seaton sampled a couple. It was hard to determine the type of the 55-year-old liquor but Rogers recalls it was likely cognac or scotch, was definitely overproof and really "hit the spot!"

Exploration deep inside the decaying wreck of *Ohio* required lights, as the slightest touch would dislodge material and stir the water into inky blackness. It was during one of their final dives that Rogers learned the hard way how dangerous wreck diving could be. Forty-five years later he remembers his "mighty close call" vividly. He was three decks down in the total darkness of one of *Ohio*'s holds and, in hindsight, far too eager to get to the treasures in a storeroom—brass navigation lamps, lanterns, chandeliers and "other fancy stuff." It almost cost him his life.

Rogers had taken a night-light diver's lamp with him but, not totally trusting the light, he had also tied a line to the dive boat. Trailing the line out behind so he could follow it back out, he proceeded down into the ship's holds. When he reached the storeroom he temporarily tied the line to a pipe, but the pipe

Built as a trans-Atlantic steamer in 1872, the *Ohio* sailed for Seattle in 1898 to take part in the Klondike gold rush. She remained operating on runs from Seattle north to Alaska right up until her loss in August 1909. She is pictured here at the coal bunkers in Nanaimo before steaming northward. VANCOUVER MARITIME MUSEUM PR 3521

Rogers and Seaton explore the bow of *Ohio*. It was here that Rogers had a "mighty close call" after being far too eager to get at the treasures in a storeroom three decks down. After losing his lifeline, and in total darkness, he was down to the last breath of air in his tank and barely made it back to the surface. FRED ROGERS COLLECTION

broke away and disappeared—with the line—into the blackness. As he groped around with his light trying to find his lifeline, Fred was keenly aware that his air supply was getting dangerously low and he was fast running out of time. He abandoned the search for the line and concentrated on trying to locate the door through which he'd entered the storeroom. Fighting off panic Rogers felt for the hull structure around him. The layout of deck beams enabled him to partially orient himself and, using his light up close, he was able to make his way along the hull plating toward what he hoped was the entrance. Fortunately he calculated correctly and was able to escape the hold and head for a dim light in the murky distance. By this time his tank was providing its last puff of air and Fred was barely able to make it to the surface.

Regardless of this near-death experience, Rogers and Seaton continued wreck diving until 1972 when they finally decided they'd had enough, sold their boat and parted ways. In just over 15 years, during any spare time they could find together, the two scuba divers had accomplished an incredible feat. They had explored much of Canada's underwater West Coast, from southern Vancouver Island to as far north as

the Alaskan border, in their search for shipwrecks. The pair accumulated so much data that, along with his detailed wreck charts, Fred Rogers was able to fill three books. The first, *Shipwrecks of British Columbia* published in 1973, was updated 20 years later with *More Shipwrecks of British Columbia*. In 2004, well into his eighties, Fred published yet another book, *Historic Divers of British Columbia*, the culmination of 50 years of research on the subject.

Even when he was well into his late eighties Fred Rogers still had projects on the go. Here he is in 2008 with one of a number of model steam engines he has built. JACQUES MARC PHOTO

Because of Rogers' meticulous work mapping and documenting BC's countless shipwrecks, the ongoing research projects carried out by the Underwater Archaeological Society of BC always commences with a phone call to the society's "diver emeritus" at his Qualicum Beach home. No use going over old ground, as chances are Fred Rogers has already "been there, done that."

# Chapter 21

# That Old Easthope Down on the Tideflats: Keeping the Easthope Engine History Alive, 2009

Ask any old-timer down on the dock what he considers to be the most famous West Coast marine engine from the first half of the twentieth century and chances are he'll reply, "Easthope." Heavy-duty, slow-turning and easy to repair, Easthopes proved a natural fit for the hundreds of "misery stick"-propelled (powered by oars) fish boats. They also happened to be the first gasoline engine to be manufactured in Vancouver, BC.

While the hundreds of Easthopes may have been the power plants of choice for the small boat fleet 75 years ago, now the only place you might come across one of these engines is in a small handful of classic craft, in a private collection or perhaps in the bilge of a long-abandoned gillnetter beached in a backwater next to an upcoast village. As artifacts from a bygone era, many of these cast-iron engines are long past any hope of restoration, and anyone who stumbles across one is often left guessing about its early history.

Today it's possible, thanks to the efforts of Joe Holmes of Richmond, to determine not only when a particular Easthope was built but also who it was originally manufactured for. It's a simple matter of retrieving the details from the engine's brass serial-number plate. Holmes was fortunate to acquire the old company records that allow him to identify each and every Easthope. Around 25 years ago he was looking for parts to keep some old Easthopes running and got in touch with Bill Easthope. Word had it that Bill had a lot of old inventory stored around his White Rock property. Once the two men realized they shared a common interest, they began buying and trading parts.

Bill Easthope happens to be the great-grandson of Ernest Easthope who, along with his sons Vincent and Ernest Junior, founded Easthope & Sons in Vancouver in the early 1900s. (Government records reveal that the partnership was formally declared on February 13, 1906.) After they sold the company and it subsequently failed, Easthope family history has it that two Easthope brothers, Percy (Peck) and Ernest Jr. (Vincent had died in 1907) bought back the name. They started up the company again in 1909 as Easthope Brothers and began manufacturing four-cycle engines. (Ernest Easthope, Jr. made a Declaration of Partnership for Easthope Brothers on February 23, 1909, as ". . . the only member of the said firm.") Their brother, George Sr., apparently joined them soon afterward.

They operated out of an Easthope Bros. shop on West Georgia Street by Coal Harbour until it closed in 1951. At that time, the whole operation was moved out to the Easthope Sales and Service outlet in Steveston, which Bill's uncle, George Easthope Jr., had opened in about 1930. (Easthope Bros. Ltd. also happened to be incorporated at this time.) Then, in 1978, when both Bill's father Gene (who had been out at Steveston since 1942) and his brother George Jr. decided they wanted to retire, the entire family-owned and operated company was sold to Ron Dodd of Richmond Machine Works on No. 2 Road in Richmond and the company name was changed to Ebros Holdings.

Now living in 100 Mile House, Bill notes that while the last Easthope gasoline engine was manufactured in 1950, the company continued manufacturing commercial fishing equipment, such as the Easthope trolling gurdies and drum-drives, for a few more years out at Steveston. Bill was working there (primarily making and repairing gurdies) when he and Dodd decided to try re-manufacturing two of the small gasoline engines (the 4–6 horsepower single cylinder and the 8–14 horsepower, single-casting twin cylinder) on their own. While they were initially encouraged by the interest in Easthope engines still out there in the fishing and pleasure boating fraternities they had to abandon the venture after a couple of years when the costs of manufacturing were found to exceed the retail prices.

This is one of the few operating Easthopes left on the coast—Al Mason's 10–18 Easthope engine in his gill-netter, *Eva*, built by the Suzuki shipyard on Annacis Island in 1937. The present two-cylinder 10–18 engine replaced the original single-cylinder Easthope in the 1950s so the boat could highball up to Rivers Inlet and elsewhere on the coast. ULRICH GAEDE PHOTO

The Steveston Sales and Service outlet ran into financial trouble in the 1980s and it all came to an end on July 31, 1987, when the company closed and the machinery and buildings were sold. As a result, a lot of what was left of the Easthope parts inventory ended up in the dumpster. Bill saved what he could but Joe says most of the "good stuff" is long gone.

Eventually, in the late 1980s, Bill told Joe (who had been buying parts from him for years), "You know, you're my best customer. Why don't you just buy everything that's left. I'm tired of this!" Bill insisted Joe take all the engine patterns too, along with most of the rest of the stuff he'd saved. Joe was reluctant at first to take the historic patterns due to the amount of care and storage he figured they'd require for proper preservation but he finally agreed to it. Bill Easthope did keep some choice parts and engines for himself, though, such as one of the only 12 "new-style" 8–14 hp engines (serial #81:5695, manufactured in 1981 and sold to D. Smith of Vancouver) and a 5–7 hp (#ZA5283, produced July 7, 1948, and sold to R.M. Rasmussen of Port Hammond, BC) that he had restored for his father. (The "new style" engines came with enclosed valve rockers and push rods.)

When Bill showed him all the old company ledgers, however, Joe got really excited and he was quick to

The *Eva's* brass engine plate confirms it as a two cylinder 10–18 Easthope. Bill Easthope says that the best way to imitate an Easthope running is to repeat "two bits, two bits, two bits . . ." To watch and actually listen to the distinctive sounds of the *Eva* and her Easthope, enter "Easthope engine running in *Eva*" into your web browser to see the videos filmed by Finn Slough photographer Ulrich Gaede. ULRICH GAEDE PHOTO

let Bill know he'd love access to the records so he could enter all the original engine and owner details into a registry on his computer. The surviving company records and patterns went all the way back to 1911 but not to the early years when the Easthope company first started out building two-cycle engines. (Joe says he has only ever seen one of these early Easthopes "in the flesh"—it was rusting away in a field.) In the end, because of the difficulty of deciphering some of the entries in the old handwritten ledgers, it took a year to painstakingly enter all the information into a computer database.

Also in the collection were the original notebooks the engine assemblers and mechanics kept in their pockets for ongoing records of each job. Even if they just tweaked an engine a little, an entry would be made in the greasy, handwritten pages. Holmes observed that the company also maintained books that kept tabs on their clientele. "They had a lot of agents and repeat customers and they would grade these guys—A, B, C, D, you know." It was a great way to keep track of who was reliable and easy to deal with and, more importantly, who was trouble or a deadbeat and rated a "D."

Joe Holmes encourages people to send him the serial numbers of Easthopes they've come across or own as collector's pieces so he can provide them with the engine's background. Every time he learns about another old Easthope still out there he adds it to the registry, but he's adamant about one thing. "I don't need any more engines! I'd just like to know what's still out there—what's alive and what's not."

If you happen to own, or know of, an old Easthope and you'd like to learn its history, contact Joe at 604-649-1270 or email him at joeholmes@shaw.ca. Joe is also an active participant on the online Old Marine Engine Discussion Board at: www.oldmarineengine.com where he answers questions on Easthope engines posted to the site.

This 15–18 Easthope is seen at George Sawchuk's Fanny Bay property on the east coast of Vancouver Island. Sawchuk paid Fanny Bay boatbuilder Martin North $100 for the engine "years ago." From the serial number (VA 4848) on the engine plaque, Joe Holmes used the old Easthope records to identify the engine as a two-cylinder 15-hp (550 rpm) completed by Easthope engine fitter V. Easthope on September 4, 1945, for the Canadian Fishing Company. RICK JAMES PHOTO, 2008

# Selective Sources & Reading

**Oral History Tapes, Rick James Collection**

Joe Quilty: September 1, 1996; Alan Heater: July 27, 1996; Fred Rogers: May 30, 2007.

**Personal Communications**

Janna Brown, Bob De Armond, Barrie McClung, Mike Burwell, Ronald A. Burke, Michael Mjelde, Barry Gough, Stanley Wardill, Ruth Masters, Ray Stockand, Bob Briggs, Newton Cameron, Fred Corneille, Norman Hacking, Glen Olson, Bill Franklin, Charles Nordin, Bob Logan, Jack Bruno, Frank Clapp, Art and Don Elworthy, Harold D. Huycke, John Henderson, Allan Heater, Joe Quilty, Mrs. R.W. Draney, Ronald A. Greene, Art Twigg, Bent Sivertz, Fred Rogers, Bill Easthope, Joe Holmes.

**Unpublished Material**

Vancouver and New Westminster Ship Registry volumes, Transport Canada. Burnaby, BC: Pacific Region Federal Records Centre, Library and Archives Canada.

Victoria Ship Registry volumes, Registry of Vessels, Transport Canada, Marine. Victoria: Transport Canada.

Vancouver Shipping Register (1890–1945). British Columbia Archives and Records Service, GR 1333, Canada, Marine Branch, reel B-2530.

**Books**

*American Lloyd's Register of British and Foreign Shipping*. American Shipmasters' Association. Available online annually to 1900. www.mysticseaport.org/library/initiative/VMSearch.cfm

Bureau of Navigation, Department of Commerce. *Merchant Vessels of the United States*. Washington, D.C.: Government Printing Office, annually.

Canada Department of Marine and Fisheries. *List of Shipping* ("Blue Book"). Ottawa: King's Printer, annually.

Canada Department of Transport. *List of Shipping* ("Blue Book"). Ottawa: Queen's Printer, annually.

E.W. Wright, ed. *Lewis & Dryden's Marine History of the Pacific Northwest*. Portland, Ore.: Lewis & Dryden Printing Co., 1895.

Gough, Barry. *Gunboat Frontier: British Maritime Authority & Northwest Coast Indians*. Vancouver: UBC Press, 1984, pp. 198–204.

Huycke, Harold D. *To Santa Rosalia Further and Back*. Newport News, Va.: The Mariner's Museum, 1970.

Lloyd's of London. *Lloyd's Register of British and Foreign Shipping*. London: Lloyd's of London, published annually since 1764.

Lubbock, Basil. *Last of the Windjammers: Volume I and II*. Glasgow: Brown, Son & Ferguson, Volume 1, 1927; Volume II, 1935.

Macpherson, Ken and John Burgess. *The Ships of Canada's Fighting Forces 1910–1993*. St. Catherine's, Ont: Vanwell Publishing, 1994.

Mitchell, W.H. and L.A. Sawyer. *British Standard Ships of World War I*. Liverpool: Sea Breezes, 1968, pp. 150–6.

Newell, Gordon, ed. *The H.W. McCurdy Marine History of the Pacific Northwest: 1895–1965*. Seattle: Superior Publishing, 1966.

Rogers, Fred. *Shipwrecks of British Columbia*. Vancouver: Douglas & MacIntyre, 1973.

Rogers, Fred. *More Shipwrecks of British Columbia*. Vancouver/Toronto: Douglas & MacIntyre, 1992.

Taylor, G.W. *Shipyards of British Columbia: The Principal Companies*. Victoria: Morriss Printing, 1986, pp. 84–93.

Twigg, Art. *Union Steamships Remembered 1920–1958*. Campbell River: A.M. Twigg, 1997.

## Selected Journal and Newspaper Articles

John MacFarlane. "Capital Iron: Scrap Dealers in Lotus Land." *Resolution: Journal of the Maritime Museum of British Columbia*, 18 February 1990, pp. 4–8.

Clapp, Frank. "British Columbia's Early Log Barges: Beginning with British Pacific Transport Company Ltd in 1924," Part I & II. *The Sea Chest: Journal of the Puget Sound Maritime Historical Society*, vol. 34, no. 3–4, March–June 2001.

James, Rick. "*Geo. S. Wright*: Part I and II." *The Sea Chest: Journal of the Puget Sound Maritime Historical Society*, vol. 44, no. 2–3, March and June 2011.

Wells, R.E. "West Coast Barges," *Victoria Daily Colonist*, 27 February 1972, pp. 12–15.

## Newspapers

19th-century US newspapers: www.infotrac.galegroup.com/itw/infomark

*Puget Sound Daily Courier.* 19, 26, 29 March 1873

*Vancouver Daily World* (1888–1924)

*Vancouver Province* (1898–)

*Vancouver Sun* (1912–)

*Victoria Daily British Colonist* (June 25 1866 – Dec 31 1886): www.britishcolonist.ca

*Victoria Daily Colonist* (Jan 1 1886–): www.britishcolonist.ca (1858–1910)

*Victoria Daily Times* (1884–)

Since this is no more than an abbreviated list, I highly recommend those looking for a more comprehensive bibliography to refer to the Underwater Archaeological Society of BC series of reports. In particular, *The Ghosts of Royston* (2004) and *Historic Shipwrecks of the Central Coast* (2010), where many of the stories in this volume were originally published in a more scholarly style and format. To order copies go to: www.uasbc.com.

# Index